REDISCOVERING

The

GODDESS

Journaling Through My Journey

to

Redefine Me

LAKEISHA FLETCHER

Published by Distinction Publishing House
Dover, Denver, Colorado
United States of America

www.distinctionpublishinghouse.com

ISBN: 979-8-9894214-4-2

This book is printed on acid-free paper.

Printed in the United States of America

Acknowledgments

Thank you to my biological mother who kept me safe as a child.

Thank you to Distinction Publishing House
for their professionalism and patience.

Thank you to my village who coached me into adulthood.

Thank you to my children who gave me great ideas
and feedback as I wrote this book.

Author's Note

I feel grateful to have Rediscovered The Goddess in me at a time when I could receive the teaching and tools of a Queen and Goddess. I am forever grateful for all of the amazing women on this journey with me and to those I have met throughout my lifetime thus far. Their gifts of sisterhood can never be replaced.

I am humble, grateful, and honored for the gift of my writing, my love for exploration, and for the use of my expansive imagination.

My poems about people, places, and things told in this book reflect feelings, experiences, and/or situations that many of us have experienced in our lifetime at some point.

I speak my truth, tell my story, and embrace my rawness through writing.

Dedication

This book is dedicated to my grandparents:
Moses Lazarus Grimes and Audrey Matilda Palmer Grimes.

Their union has taught me that love cannot be defined;
instead,
LOVE is lived…
LOVE is learned…
and LOVE can be a discovery with every new relationship.

Table of Contents

Introduction

Self-discovery happened unexpectedly, or at least it felt like it as I started my poetic journaling experience in Rediscovering The Goddess in me. Throughout my high school years, I found peace and serenity in my writings that lasted throughout my adulthood. My creativity came to life through my poems. Today, I share my original pieces of written art with you.

To begin, I knew what was happening when I became someone's daughter. I listened to my mother, attended school, and made good grades as told. I knew what was happening when I received the name of "honors & graduated student" naturally after I graduated from my alma mater, Tennessee State University (TSU). I knew what was happening when I became someone's little sister. I had someone to play with, someone to talk to, and someone to fight with, as well. I knew what was happening when I became someone's mother. Naturally, I embraced this role after the birth of my handsome, beautiful browned-skinned son and radiant, joyful, beautiful browned-skinned daughter. I knew what was happening when I became someone's aunt. I spoiled my nieces and nephews in all of the best ways possible, whenever possible. Lastly, I knew what was happening when I received the name "wife" after accepting a diamond ring from my first husband of twelve years and eight years of courtship, totaling a beautiful twenty-year union.

However, I did not know what was happening when I lost my pleasure. I did not understand what was happening when I received the name "divorcee." I did not know what was happening when I lost to death my father, my brother, my grandfather, and my grandmother (who was a second mother to me). In no way did I know what was happening when I lost close friendships and I definitely did not understand what was happening when I lost my Goddess glow. Yet, I somehow knew how to neglect my inner being and to forget to find pleasure in life during my time of rupture. Things were happening to me and all around me. I was changing, evolving, and getting burned out fast. Hence, more ruptures came, and my burnout was real. I forgot the Goddess code and forgot my vows to love myself. So, naturally, I retreated, turned inward, and began journaling.

Poetic journaling to me, was and still is my form of therapy. This form of therapy allows me and many other individuals the opportunity to be truthful and honest with themselves. For me, my poetic journaling journey began in high school and then stopped. I started again after attending a Goddess Retreat where my awakening to rediscover the Goddess was a fruitful one.

I trusted the actions and reactions of my ancestors who came before me. Meaning, I trusted my ancestors knowing how to raise me, how to bring life back into me, and how to thrive, not just survive, in this world. I trusted my parents, grandparents, authority figures, and influencers who were my role models as I rediscovered myself. I trusted the elderly knew how to give me hope, a future, and a renewed life in my rupture. I trusted the universe knew how to give me my purpose, how to love me, and how to show others how to love me in my rediscovery.

And with this information I journaled. From childhood into adulthood, I learned my likes and dislikes. For example, I liked the color green. However, I wouldn't say I liked geometry. I understood myself very well; yet, somewhere in life, between ages thirty and forty years old, I got distracted and lost myself. I misplaced what I had understood.

As I journaled, I naturally stepped into the next best thing which was to speak and live my truth again. I began to heal, reconnect, and remove any distractions from my growth. I implemented new skills while learning to be grounded again. At the same time, during this experience, I felt the need to be connected and disconnected from the outside world, so that's what I did, without stopping my journaling.

I created my own women's circle called the SistaGurlLounge (SGL). The SGL started after my successful completion of a women's leadership seminar. It was another awakening for me, and I was truly ready to be emancipated from my peer's judgmental glaze. As a result, I was officially practicing the art of pleasure and redefining myself while removing unproductive thoughts and negative generational patterns. The group setting I created for myself was for unfiltered truth and honesty. Just like that, I became a student again and regained myself. Between my women's circle and poetic journaling journey, I journaled for a total of eighty-eight days to assist me in writing this book and deliberately chose to think about my decisions, remove the victim story from my vocabulary, and celebrate life's changes. I aggressively reminded myself of all that I had changed over the years and those things and people that had removed themselves from my life that did not serve me any longer. Through this transition, my objective was to not play myself small because I knew that would only lead to destructive behavior; rather, I found how to become larger than life resulting in me becoming an uncaged, untamed, and rediscovered Goddess.

In my nakedness of being untamed, unleased, not caged, and unapologetic, I was led by eight delicious desires. Come with me on my journey from the last moments of high school with friends into my lively years of adulthood which include relationships, heartbreaks, revelations, and a full array of emotions that come with it. From the deaths of friends and family to happiness found in the birth of new things people and places, and all of the things in between, I dedicate my poetic journal to my honesty, my truth, and the vulnerability it takes to be me, unapologetically as I share my desires with you and rediscover my Goddess.

DESIRE 1: FUN AND PLEASURE – I desire to be full of love and forgiveness, know my self-worth, and maintain a consistent and reliable relationship with my children. I desire for all interactions with others to be mentally, physically, emotionally, spiritually healthy, and filled with laughter. I desire to stay in my pleasure. I desire to have fun every day. I desire to always be beautifully untamed and unapologetic in speaking my truth.

DESIRE 2: SELF-APPROVAL - I desire to feel and believe I am right in my body and thoughts. I desire not to be afraid of my potential as a Queen and a Goddess.

DESIRE 3: SELF-FORGIVENESS - I desire to have mindful responses. I desire to think before I speak when answering questions that are coming from my children and those I care about. I desire not to take people's thoughts opinions and perspectives personally. I desire always to remember to forgive, and that people make mistakes. I desire to be non-judgmental to myself and others around me. I desire not to take anything or anyone I care about for granted and to be grateful always for everything positive and good-natured.

DESIRE 4: RESTORATIVE RELATIONSHIPS - I desire to increase my effective communication level with family members, including my siblings. I desire to stay connected to my family. I desire a peaceful and renewing relationship with past friends, family members, and colleagues.

DESIRE 5: PEACE and GUIDANCE - I desire to listen more and talk less in relationships. I desire discernment. I desire to co-parent in a way that shows we love our children unconditionally. I desire to co-parent peacefully.

DESIRE 7: LOVE, WISDOM AND DISCERNMENT - I desire to fully accept, acknowledge, and appreciate my new husband and male best friend. I desire the knowledge to navigate all future relationships into a space that is fruitful, faithful, loyal, open, honest, helpful, and 100% reciprocal of peace.

DESIRE 8: WEALTH - I desire endless cash flow, endless wisdom, and an excellent memory always. I desire to receive it while remaining humble. I desire to learn from past experiences that will enhance my future experiences to be a stronger, wiser, healthier Goddess and Queen.

As you take this journey with me, I am honored and grateful you joined me. Within the next eighty-eight days, I show consistency and self-discipline within my daily routine, activities, and events for the day, which includes:

- Exercising, showering or rinsing my naked body with clean, cool, flowing water;
- Oil body or massage body, reading and writing my desires, sixty seconds of self-approval through positive affirmations, and three minutes of self-acceptance by dancing in the mirror naked;
- Getting dressed (be sure to pay attention to clothing items that are clean, comfortable, and sexy (or another adjective that makes you feel good);
- Drinking one glass of water (minimum) and listening to a song from my playlist;
- Create or write positive affirmations;
- Eat breakfast (with hot or iced tea);
- Make a pleasure list for the day (see below), and throughout the day, remember to flirt, play, and have fun; and
- At the end of my morning routine, I journaled my gratitude(s), constructed a poem and/or mantra, stated an affirmation, and created a pleasure list to begin visualizing my day:

EXAMPLE:

Day 1 Events: Visualize your day (3 or more connections with self): Take a nap, drink water, practice outdoor yoga, write a poem;

Day 1 Pleasure list: Spend time with children, clean my home, take a nature walk; and

Day 1 Reflection: What came through from me today? I must allow myself to be patient, to be content, and to be confident in knowing I am enough. I am making the right steps towards my truth.

I will take you through my daily practices where I become awakened and enlightened. In these practices, I set my intentions to improve my overall well-being. Now, I invite you to list your eight desires which you would like to manifest by the end of this journey. So go grab a writing utensil and get ready for the next eighty-eight days of rediscovering your Goddess.

Let's begin…

Desire 1:

_____
_____
_____
_____
_____
_____
_____
_____
_____.

Desire 2:

_____
_____
_____
_____
_____
_____
_____
_____
_____.

Desire 3:

_____
_____
_____
_____
_____
_____
_____
_____
_____.

Desire 4:

_____

_____

_____

_____

_____

_____

_____

_____

_____.

Desire 5:

_____

_____

_____

_____

_____

_____

_____

_____

_____

_____.

Desire 6:

_____
_____
_____
_____
_____
_____
_____
_____
_____
_____.

Desire 7:

_____
_____
_____
_____
_____
_____
_____
_____
_____
_____.

Desire 8:

_____

_____

_____

_____

_____

_____

_____

_____

_____ .

Day 1
Affirmation: I Am Enough

Welcome

My book of poems is written here
For all of you who have shed a tear

My poems are true
Some might make you blue

Real words for the soul
Only to make you whole

Some are to brighten the day
Written for the happy and gay

Others might speak to you
And make your old outlook new

In no particular order, I present to you
My book of poems written especially for you

Daily Gratitude:

_____
_____
_____
_____
_____
_____.

Pleasure List For Today (Things to Do, Desires & Other Note(s)):

_____
_____
_____
_____
_____
_____.

Today's Affirmation:

_____
_____
_____
_____
_____
_____
_____.

Visualize Your Day:

_____
_____
_____
_____
_____
_____
_____.

Non-Pleasures of Today (Things to Do Tomorrow, Drama(s) of The Day, Possible Failures & Do-Overs):

_____
_____
_____
_____
_____
_____
_____.

Reflections From Today:

_____
_____
_____
_____
_____
_____
_____
_____.

Day 2
Affirmation: I Am Curious

Contemplating, Watching, & Spinning My Wheels

She came from a dark place
Where the murk and mud had her feeling stuck
She sat in a lonely place, feeling down, loneliness and in a rut
She had made her home a place of peace and a sanctuary
Yet, with the wrong company, it turned into a hut
A place of shambles it had become
An asylum almost, that the inmates would run
Medications free flowing, but no one taking none
And the playroom once full of laughter was no more fun
A sad little girl running from her fears
Eye burning and eyesight blurry because of the tears
A sad place for a sad girl because she came from the dark
Where the murk and mud had her feeling stuck

Daily Gratitude:

_____

_____

_____

_____

_____

_____.

Pleasure List For Today (Things to Do, Desires & Other Note(s)):

_____

_____

_____

_____

_____

_____.

Today's Affirmation:

_____

_____

_____

_____

_____

_____

_____.

Visualize Your Day:

_____
_____
_____
_____
_____
_____.

Non-Pleasures of Today (Things to Do Tomorrow, Drama(s) of The Day, Possible Failures & Do-Overs):

_____
_____
_____
_____
_____.

Reflections From Today:

_____
_____
_____
_____
_____
_____
_____.

Day 3
Affirmation: Today I Will Open My Mind To New Possibilities

My 18th Birthday

This day has been a good day
It has been a very good day
For I can see that the Lord is blessing me
In every way there is to be

One more year older
Another year with new growth
Another year of experience to share
One more year that I was blessed to live and be here

Another birthday, an older me has arrived
Another birthday that I have spent with the ones I love
This day is used as a symbol
That I am destined to survive without fear or trembles!

Daily Gratitude:

_____

_____

_____

_____

_____

_____.

Pleasure List For Today (Things to Do, Desires & Other Note(s)):

_____

_____

_____

_____

_____

_____.

Today's Affirmation:

_____

_____

_____

_____

_____

_____

_____.

Visualize Your Day:

_____

_____

_____

_____

_____

_____.

Non-Pleasures of Today (Things to Do Tomorrow, Drama(s) of The Day, Possible Failures & Do-Overs):

_____

_____

_____

_____

_____

_____.

Reflections From Today:

_____

_____

_____

_____

_____

_____.

Day 4
Affirmation: I Am Special

Why Worry

Why worry about the past
About what happens, when it happens
Events in order, first to last?

Why worry and ask why it went that way
We can't change the way it turned out
So what else is there to say?

However, you may think that it's for the best
To act on impulse
Without thinking about the rest!

Instead of thinking about what could be
You let your ego get in the way
And said the hell with me

But you were not able to let me go
You couldn't get me out of your head
Now what does that go to show?

Well, it shows me how much you've grown
How much you really care
And to that I say, Why Worry
Because now you're the one shedding the tear!

Daily Gratitude:

_____

_____

_____

_____

_____

_____.

Pleasure List For Today (Things to Do, Desires & Other Note(s)):

_____

_____

_____

_____

_____

_____.

Today's Affirmation:

_____

_____

_____

_____

_____

_____

_____.

Visualize Your Day:

_____
_____
_____
_____
_____
_____.

Non-Pleasures of Today (Things to Do Tomorrow, Drama(s) of The Day, Possible Failures & Do-Overs):

_____
_____
_____
_____
_____
_____.

Reflections From Today:

_____
_____
_____
_____
_____
_____
_____.

Day 5
Affirmation: I Am Unique

Celebration Time

Happy Mother's Day, Happy Birthday Day,
Happy Serenity Day
Peace and blessings to me
I'm learning to party with me
I'm learning to let things be
I'm stretching and growing into a better me
Today, I celebrate a brand new me

Happy Mother's Day, Happy Birthday Day,
Happy Serenity Day
Peace and blessings to me
I'm growing with endless possibilities
I'm growing like a budding tree
I'm moving, flying, exploring like a bumble bee
I am earth, wind, fire….
I am the flow of water in the sea

Happy Mother's Day, Happy Birthday Day,
Happy Serenity Day
Peace and blessings to me
Grace and mercy, love and forgiveness surround me
I am moving, I am changing,
I am ever-evolving into a new me
I am swimming, I am running,
I am walking that path that defines me

Happy Mother's Day, Happy Birthday Day,
Happy Serenity Day
Peace and blessings to me

Daily Gratitude:

_____

_____

_____

_____

_____

_____.

Pleasure List For Today (Things to Do, Desires & Other Note(s)):

_____

_____

_____

_____

_____

_____.

Today's Affirmation:

_____

_____

_____

_____

_____

_____

_____.

Visualize Your Day:

_____
_____
_____
_____
_____
_____.

Non-Pleasures of Today (Things to Do Tomorrow, Drama(s) of The Day, Possible Failures & Do-Overs):

_____
_____
_____
_____
_____
_____.

Reflections From Today:

_____
_____
_____
_____
_____
_____
_____.

Day 6
Affirmation: I Am Mindful

Thank You

Thank you for always being there
Thank you for always showing that you care
Thank you for spending time with me
Thank you for always being near

Having someone in my life
That has done so much for me
Means that you not only love me
But have shown me a successful key

A key that will open many doors
A key that will show me the path to take
A key that gives me determination
A key that will help with the decisions I must make

It is not easy
To find a person like you
Someone to come home to at night
And say I love you too

This person whom I call my mother
Is a special lady indeed
A lady with love and support to give
A lady who can give to my needs

To my mother, I love you so
May God bless you from your head to your toe
May he always keep you in his heart
So that we will never be too far apart, Mother, thank you

Daily Gratitude:

_____
_____
_____
_____
_____
_____.

Pleasure List For Today (Things to Do, Desires & Other Note(s)):

_____
_____
_____
_____
_____
_____.

Today's Affirmation:

_____
_____
_____
_____
_____
_____
_____.

Visualize Your Day:

_____
_____
_____
_____
_____
_____.

Non-Pleasures of Today (Things to Do Tomorrow, Drama(s) of The Day, Possible Failures & Do-Overs):

_____
_____
_____
_____
_____
_____.

Reflections From Today:

_____
_____
_____
_____
_____
_____.

Day 7
Affirmation: I Am Peaceful

Someone Special

It is alright if he messes up
Don't matter if he breaks my favorite cup

At the club, he may dance as he pleases
If he forgets his, I don't mind him using my keys

I don't mind walking down the street
Because that is where he decided for us to meet

Washing his clothes is just fine by me
Him not forgetting to leave me some money

Because I have someone special in my life
Someone special who's really nice

Don't mind going to work and coming home to cook
And, it doesn't bother me that he doesn't watch TV
But rather we snuggle to read a good book

When the nights are cold, I let him turn on the heat
Making sure that he wraps me up with the covers, nice and neat

I don't care if he needs to work late in the night
And when he comes home, there is no need to fight

Because I have someone special in my life
Someone special that's really nice

Daily Gratitude:

_____

_____

_____

_____

_____

_____.

Pleasure List For Today (Things to Do, Desires & Other Note(s)):

_____

_____

_____

_____

_____.

Today's Affirmation:

_____

_____

_____

_____

_____

_____.

Visualize Your Day:

_____

_____

_____

_____

_____

_____.

Non-Pleasures of Today (Things to Do Tomorrow, Drama(s) of The Day, Possible Failures & Do-Overs):

_____

_____

_____

_____

_____

_____.

Reflections From Today:

_____

_____

_____

_____

_____

_____

_____.

Day 8
Affirmation: I Am Happy

Yesterday

Now I know it is finally over
No more wishing on a four-leaf clover

Hoping that we will be
All while you were abusing me

Verbally with words that I did not hear
At the same time, I was wiping away salty tears

Who was I to tell?
That our relationship was going to hell
Having bad moods with hurtful tunes

All coming from your lips
Not once making up with a kiss

Wasn't it fun while it lasted?
Trying not to think about our sorry ass past

Putting up with things that I said I wouldn't
Doing things that I shouldn't

First impressions, thinking of you as a mate
Not even having a first date
Having feelings for you all still while loving you

Yesterday
Cont'd

Not thinking about what to say
What you did not do and what did not happen in May

It seems so sad for me to say
That I still have those feelings for you

I was the one and still in love with you
As time passes, the feelings will too
The excitement will rise of me finding someone new

To treat me like the Queen I was brought up to be
Having renewable strength, courage, and wisdom inside of me

Daily Gratitude:

_____
_____
_____
_____
_____
_____.

Pleasure List For Today (Things to Do, Desires & Other Note(s)):

_____
_____
_____
_____
_____
_____.

Today's Affirmation:

_____
_____
_____
_____
_____
_____
_____.

Visualize Your Day:

_____

_____

_____

_____

_____

_____.

Non-Pleasures of Today (Things to Do Tomorrow, Drama(s) of The Day, Possible Failures & Do-Overs):

_____

_____

_____

_____

_____

_____.

Reflections From Today:

_____

_____

_____

_____

_____

_____

_____.

Day 9
Affirmation: I Trust Myself

The Games We Play

We laugh and talk
We make jokes as we walk

I call and you are here
Don't mind waiting for you anywhere

Not knowing what to say
But thinking that I love you in every single way

Wanting to be around you
Thinking that I love you

Instead, I love that game
A game where I have you tamed

To mode you into what I want you to be
Which is to only think of me

So when you finally do decide to leave
I will be able to let you be

Because you would only know of me
And eventually, you'll be asking again for my key

Daily Gratitude:

_____
_____
_____
_____
_____
_____.

Pleasure List For Today (Things to Do, Desires & Other Note(s)):

_____
_____
_____
_____
_____
_____.

Today's Affirmation:

_____
_____
_____
_____
_____
_____
_____.

Visualize Your Day:

_____

_____

_____

_____

_____

_____.

**Non-Pleasures of Today (Things to Do Tomorrow, Drama(s) of
The Day, Possible Failures & Do-Overs):**

_____

_____

_____

_____

_____

_____.

Reflections From Today:

_____

_____

_____

_____

_____

_____

_____.

Day 10
Affirmation: I Am Resilent

Missing You

Feelings that I shouldn't have
For a male like you
Comes along so fast
There is no time to slow down
To see if those feelings are true
You say you care; you won't let anything hurt me
You say you can't show your feelings because
Of your past experiences

In exchange, I show and tell you mine
Hoping not to regret what I have just said
I'm loving you but not telling you
I don't know if these feelings are mutual
Listening to songs that remind me of you
Hating the feeling of being played with
Hating the silence of not talking to you

How could you damage me so
Trying my best for you not to get too close
Too many feelings and emotions
Are going through my mind and body
Friends telling me of the things they see
That are blind to me
Family telling you to keep away from me
Too many feelings for one male
This male that makes me smile and be happy
When I'm supposed to be mad

Missing You

Cont'd

The same male that makes me laugh and cry
Trying to push him away from me
But pulling back to try again
I try not to get close

I back away but he draws me closer
You hold me close and whisper loving things to me
You take me in, I'm guessing you love me
Yet, You seldom tell me

Why can't I let go and let you be?
Are you playing games?
I turn to walk away,
But still thinking about you and me
And me still missing you

Daily Gratitude:

_____

_____

_____

_____

_____

_____.

Pleasure List For Today (Things to Do, Desires & Other Note(s)):

_____

_____

_____

_____

_____

_____.

Today's Affirmation:

_____

_____

_____

_____

_____

_____

_____.

Visualize Your Day:

_____
_____
_____
_____
_____
_____.

Non-Pleasures of Today (Things to Do Tomorrow, Drama(s) of The Day, Possible Failures & Do-Overs):

_____
_____
_____
_____
_____
_____.

Reflections From Today:

_____
_____
_____
_____
_____
_____
_____.

Day 11

Affirmation: I Am Friendly

A Best Friend

I've had many of friends
Some whom my mother did not like
But recently I met this girl
A sister, a pal, a really good friend

It is not everyday
That you can meet someone to care for
Someone to trust and talk to
Someone who would always be there

I have this friend
Who is my best friend
She is above the rest of my peers
Just like a sister, she really cares

She is a part of the family
Just like my mother's own child
She is warm, kind, and loving
Sincere with an attitude that's mild

We did not know each other very long
And when we met, we did not connect
We grew from each other and I love her so
And that is why she is my best friend
Above everyone else I know

Daily Gratitude:

_____

_____

_____

_____

_____

_____.

Pleasure List For Today (Things to Do, Desires & Other Note(s)):

_____

_____

_____

_____

_____

_____.

Today's Affirmation:

_____

_____

_____

_____

_____

_____

_____

_____.

Visualize Your Day:

_____

_____

_____

_____

_____

_____.

Non-Pleasures of Today (Things to Do Tomorrow, Drama(s) of The Day, Possible Failures & Do-Overs):

_____

_____

_____

_____

_____

_____.

Reflections From Today:

_____

_____

_____

_____

_____

_____

_____.

Day 12
Affirmation: I Am Healthy

Don't Look

Don't look too hard at my face
Remember what you said about moving too fast,
At a certain pace, you had it
But didn't know what to do
So now I am singing that old love song right back to you

Don't look too hard at my sexy waist
Looking further down and remembering how it tastes
No more hugs and kisses goodbye
No one helping you with your tie

Don't look so closely at the ring on my fingers
You had your chance but you chose neither

Don't look too hard at my lower back
Just make sure that all your shit is packed

Don't look too hard at my door keys, car, or bank accounts
No more wondering what we were all about

So don't look too hard at the past and our old love
As you already know the shit did not last
Bye-bye to you as you fly away like a wounded dove

Daily Gratitude:

_____

_____

_____

_____

_____

_____.

Pleasure List For Today (Things to Do, Desires & Other Note(s)):

_____

_____

_____

_____

_____

_____.

Today's Affirmation:

_____

_____

_____

_____

_____

_____.

Visualize Your Day:

_____
_____
_____
_____
_____
_____.

Non-Pleasures of Today (Things to Do Tomorrow, Drama(s) of The Day, Possible Failures & Do-Overs):

_____
_____
_____
_____
_____.

Reflections From Today:

_____
_____
_____
_____
_____
_____.

Day 13
Affirmation: I Am Affluent

Life

The reading of these poems
Is not hard to understand
It sets the norm
For other ideas to be unborn
and some other things left torn

Torn wide open, yet doors never closed
Words unspoken, yet questions still posed…
Like, "Why did he really leave"….
And "Why didn't I stay"
Like, "Why couldn't I let it be"
And, "Was it really worth losing me"

Seems just like yesterday
We were all just hanging out
Now we have to really find out
What life is all about

We must take life seriously
Because it is not a game
We must take careful steps
Just like when a tiger is being tamed

People come and go so very fast
Just like a car which can eventually run of out gas
There are no returns after a person dies
All we can say is our goodbyes
While wearing those expensive but not priceless suits and ties

Daily Gratitude:

_____

_____

_____

_____

_____

_____.

Pleasure List For Today (Things to Do, Desires & Other Note(s)):

_____

_____

_____

_____

_____

_____.

Today's Affirmation:

_____

_____

_____

_____

_____

_____

_____.

Visualize Your Day:

_____

_____

_____

_____

_____

_____.

Non-Pleasures of Today (Things to Do Tomorrow, Drama(s) of The Day, Possible Failures & Do-Overs):

_____

_____

_____

_____

_____

_____.

Reflections From Today:

_____

_____

_____

_____

_____

_____

_____.

Day 14
Affirmation: I Am Responsible

Love

Simple questions I ask myself
Why I take the time out
To listen to this bullshit you tell me
Day after day, round and about

Memories of the first time
When we were reunited
Made me happy because I
Thought you were mine and you
Would be confident and trustworthy

They say, "The past is the past"
I say "My present contains my future"
Looking at what happened and what could have been
But was futureless
There's nothing else to say
But goodbye

Daily Gratitude:

_____
_____
_____
_____
_____
_____.

Pleasure List For Today (Things to Do, Desires & Other Note(s)):

_____
_____
_____
_____
_____
_____.

Today's Affirmation:

_____
_____
_____
_____
_____
_____
_____.

Visualize Your Day:

_____
_____
_____
_____
_____
_____.

Non-Pleasures of Today (Things to Do Tomorrow, Drama(s) of The Day, Possible Failures & Do-Overs):

_____
_____
_____
_____
_____
_____.

Reflections From Today:

_____
_____
_____
_____
_____
_____
_____.

Day 15
Affirmation: I Am Adventurous

Never Ending

Walking and talking is what we did
All while thinking about getting back in bed

Getting up for work without leaving for a kiss
Knowing that both of us would be missed

Could not wait to get home to see your handsome face
Not ever realizing we were moving at a fast pace

Loving you more every day that would pass
Not ever fighting or breaking any glass

Loving the way you hold me, kiss me and more
Hating to see you leave out the door

Not worrying when you would return
Because I know that days with you, our love is earned

Daily Gratitude:

_____

_____

_____

_____

_____

_____.

Pleasure List For Today (Things to Do, Desires & Other Note(s)):

_____

_____

_____

_____

_____

_____.

Today's Affirmation:

_____

_____

_____

_____

_____

_____

_____.

Visualize Your Day:

_____
_____
_____
_____
_____
_____.

Non-Pleasures of Today (Things to Do Tomorrow, Drama(s) of The Day, Possible Failures & Do-Overs):

_____
_____
_____
_____
_____
_____.

Reflections From Today:

_____
_____
_____
_____
_____
_____
_____.

Day 16
Affirmation: I Am Trustworthy

Top it Off

I let you in and loved you till the end
But you abused what you had and now you sit around looking mad

Confused about the past and there's no hope for the future
But still telling your friends that it will take no time
To get another girl that suits ya!

It's funny how mature you can act with your boys
But when I come home all you want to do is play with your toys

And to top it off, you say that you don't care what happens
But it didn't matter because I was the captain

I directed the way and you did as I say
So now it's time to go because I don't want you anymore

It must be funny for me to leave after so many years
Moving my bags while wiping away the tears

Until we meet again, best wishes to you my friend
And to top it off, I really did have true feelings for you
Remembering what we've experienced till the end with a frown

Daily Gratitude:

_____

_____

_____

_____

_____

_____.

Pleasure List For Today (Things to Do, Desires & Other Note(s)):

_____

_____

_____

_____

_____

_____.

Today's Affirmation:

_____

_____

_____

_____

_____

_____

_____.

Visualize Your Day:

_____
_____
_____
_____
_____
_____ .

Non-Pleasures of Today (Things to Do Tomorrow, Drama(s) of The Day, Possible Failures & Do-Overs):

_____
_____
_____
_____
_____
_____ .

Reflections From Today:

_____
_____
_____
_____
_____
_____
_____ .

Day 17
Affirmation: I Am Kind To Myself & Others

My Old Life

I would love to have it back
The days when life didn't seem so rough
I would enjoy having those friendships again
Maybe then life would feel so tough

I would love to have it back
The wedding bells and big white house
I would enjoy having company over and late-night parties
With no objections, just sitting cute and quiet like a mouse

I would love to have it back
But is that what I really want to do
Would I enjoy not being me, not speaking up proudly?
I want it back but would it be true?

What I had is now gone, not lost
What I want is here now, no cost
What I hope to have in the future, is neither here nor there
And what I desire to have later is my peace, which is no longer rare

Daily Gratitude:

_____

_____

_____

_____

_____

_____.

Pleasure List For Today (Things to Do, Desires & Other Note(s)):

_____

_____

_____

_____

_____

_____.

Today's Affirmation:

_____

_____

_____

_____

_____

_____

_____.

Visualize Your Day:

_____

_____

_____

_____

_____

_____.

Non-Pleasures of Today (Things to Do Tomorrow, Drama(s) of The Day, Possible Failures & Do-Overs):

_____

_____

_____

_____

_____

_____.

Reflections From Today:

_____

_____

_____

_____

_____

_____

_____.

Day 18
Affirmation: I Am Bold

Bored AF

Nothing to do so I am writing to you
There are no people to talk to
Or no one to cheer up because they're all blue

Bored as hell, and can't wait to hear a bell
An alarm or some signal letting me know it's time to go

So tired that I need some sleep
Maybe I will try counting sheep

And if that does not help
I'll start counting the holes in my belt

About three more hours until I am free
No more pretending and acting like I am busy as a bee

Bored as hell with nothing else to do but as long as I'm getting paid
Ain't got much time to complain

Nothing to do so I am writing to you
About to tell you about the time I spent counting hundreds of dimes

Anything will do
Instead of sitting here without you

Daily Gratitude:

_____
_____
_____
_____
_____
_____.

Pleasure List For Today (Things to Do, Desires & Other Note(s)):

_____
_____
_____
_____
_____
_____.

Today's Affirmation:

_____
_____
_____
_____
_____
_____
_____.

Visualize Your Day:

_____

_____

_____

_____

_____

_____.

Non-Pleasures of Today (Things to Do Tomorrow, Drama(s) of The Day, Possible Failures & Do-Overs):

_____

_____

_____

_____

_____

_____.

Reflections From Today:

_____

_____

_____

_____

_____

_____

_____.

Day 19
Affirmation: I Am Audacious

Maple Tree

Hey there little bubble bee
Why do you continuously circle round this old ass maple tree
It looks old and it has died
Silly little bumble bee, don't continue to try

That old ass maple tree bears no more sweetness
For its taste is no longer sweet
The leaves have withered
It has gone to sleep

Hey there little bumble bee, don't fly so fast looking for it again
The season has gone and the maple has dried up
You tasted it once and now it is gone
Don't weep, don't cry
You've done nothing wrong
For the season has passed and it is time to move on

Hey there little bubble bee, looks like you're a little tired
Don't be a fool and refuse to be schooled
If I told you once, I told you twice
This old ass maple tree no longer tastes so nice
So move from here, let the taste be of a sweet memory

Fly away little bubble bee with your divinity
That dried-up maple tree is old and it has died
Silly little bumble bee
Get up and move on
And let that old ass maple tree fall to the waste side

Daily Gratitude:

_____
_____
_____
_____
_____
_____.

Pleasure List For Today (Things to Do, Desires & Other Note(s)):

_____
_____
_____
_____
_____.

Today's Affirmation:

_____
_____
_____
_____
_____
_____.

Visualize Your Day:

_____

_____

_____

_____

_____

_____.

Non-Pleasures of Today (Things to Do Tomorrow, Drama(s) of The Day, Possible Failures & Do-Overs):

_____

_____

_____

_____

_____

_____.

Reflections From Today:

_____

_____

_____

_____

_____

_____

_____.

Day 20
Affirmation: I Am Astonishing

Making Time

Busy….
No time to make time
Never in the house
Never answer the phone
Leaving messages, but no returned calls

Hearing bullshit from you day and night
Jealously taking over, wanting a new lifestyle
Us being so young, I'm thinking you might
Go off and find someone else, whom I don't approve

Time is made for us to spend together
Loving you without the sex
Thinking of you day and night
Wanting you, hoping everything will turn out alright

Being taken on roller coaster rides
Can no longer sit and look out at the tides
Time to go and become busy again
Even the hugs and kisses came to an end

While you're so busy
Time for me to stop growing old
Time to get out and be youthful again
So don't worry about me, I'm busy…I'm gone

Daily Gratitude:

_____

_____

_____

_____

_____

_____.

Pleasure List For Today (Things to Do, Desires & Other Note(s)):

_____

_____

_____

_____

_____

_____.

Today's Affirmation:

_____

_____

_____

_____

_____

_____

_____.

Visualize Your Day:

_____

_____

_____

_____

_____

_____.

Non-Pleasures of Today (Things to Do Tomorrow, Drama(s) of The Day, Possible Failures & Do-Overs):

_____

_____

_____

_____

_____.

Reflections From Today:

_____

_____

_____

_____

_____

_____

_____.

Day 21
Affirmation: I Am Brave

Crazy Thoughts

What are these feelings that we feel?
Do I love you?
Will this turn into a sex thing?
I plan to wait until I am married
Leave now!

Don't think that you can change me
I thought that this was real
You need to tell me what you expect from me
I told you what I wanted

I love the time we spend together
I love being around you in your arms
The feelings that no one else give to me
The feelings that you let me feel

Yet, what is up with you?
The roller coaster rides that I go on with you
I use to want to learn you
I am starting to care less about you

Do what you want
It doesn't even matter anymore
Call me if you want
Let me know what's up with us

I guess I'll see or talk to you whenever
But let me know before it's too late for you.
Stay happy, I sure will.

Daily Gratitude:

_____

_____

_____

_____

_____

_____.

Pleasure List For Today (Things to Do, Desires & Other Note(s)):

_____

_____

_____

_____

_____

_____.

Today's Affirmation:

_____

_____

_____

_____

_____

_____

_____.

Visualize Your Day:

_____

_____

_____

_____

_____

_____.

**Non-Pleasures of Today (Things to Do Tomorrow, Drama(s) of
The Day, Possible Failures & Do-Overs):**

_____

_____

_____

_____

_____

_____.

Reflections From Today:

_____

_____

_____

_____

_____

_____

_____.

Day 22
Affirmation: I Am Problem-Solver

High School Blues

Pregnancy, It's not for me!
I only have one more year in school
Why throw it all away now
The other years have been great
With no babies to carry around

I see my friends with their children
Happy as can be
For their playtime is over now
Because they have to pick up their children at three

It may look easy from the outside
But babies take a lot from you
Wait till you have a baby and you are not ready
…..you will be saying those words too

So to my young females out there….
Word to the wise, wait till you are ready
Don't listen to what he says
Because you will be the one pregnant
And having the baby nine months from today

Daily Gratitude:

_____
_____
_____
_____
_____
_____.

Pleasure List For Today (Things to Do, Desires & Other Note(s)):

_____
_____
_____
_____
_____
_____.

Today's Affirmation:

_____
_____
_____
_____
_____
_____.

Visualize Your Day:

_____
_____
_____
_____
_____
_____.

Non-Pleasures of Today (Things to Do Tomorrow, Drama(s) of The Day, Possible Failures & Do-Overs):

_____
_____
_____
_____
_____
_____.

Reflections From Today:

_____
_____
_____
_____
_____
_____
_____.

Day 23
Affirmation: I Am Optimistic

The Church

What can I say
About the church people today
How they love and praise the lord
And want their life to be ever more

I lay down on my bed
And think about the bible and what was read
How much do these people really believe in that man?
How they can't say what they believe and take a stand

There isn't much that I can say
About these false prophets today
Just stay true to yourself and your heart
Don't follow the wrong, be smart

Daily Gratitude:

_____

_____

_____

_____

_____

_____.

Pleasure List For Today (Things to Do, Desires & Other Note(s)):

_____

_____

_____

_____

_____

_____.

Today's Affirmation:

_____

_____

_____

_____

_____

_____

_____.

Visualize Your Day:

_____

_____

_____

_____

_____

_____ .

Non-Pleasures of Today (Things to Do Tomorrow, Drama(s) of The Day, Possible Failures & Do-Overs):

_____

_____

_____

_____

_____

_____ .

Reflections From Today:

_____

_____

_____

_____

_____

_____

_____ .

Day 24
Affirmation: I Am Attractive

Valentine's Day

I'll see how much you really care
When I don't get a card or chocolates to share

I'll see how much you really care
when I ask for you and you are not there

I'll see how much you really care
when I give you your gifts to say I care
and all you do is give me a glimpse and not even a stare

Daily Gratitude:

_____
_____
_____
_____
_____
_____.

Pleasure List For Today (Things to Do, Desires & Other Note(s)):

_____
_____
_____
_____
_____
_____.

Today's Affirmation:

_____
_____
_____
_____
_____
_____.

Visualize Your Day:

_____

_____

_____

_____

_____

_____.

Non-Pleasures of Today (Things to Do Tomorrow, Drama(s) of The Day, Possible Failures & Do-Overs):

_____

_____

_____

_____

_____.

Reflections From Today:

_____

_____

_____

_____

_____

_____

_____.

Day 25
Affirmation: I Am Resourceful

Speechless

When there's no more words to be spoken
When the conversation has ceased,
And the music record sounds like it has broken
After the sun goes down and the moon comes up
When the entire wine bottle is empty
And there's no more to fill up the cup
That's when you'll know I'm speechless

When your side of the bed is no longer warm
When that shirt you brought is now unrecognized, dirty, and torn
After the movie has ended and the credits play on the screen
When the mere sight of your face makes me want to scream
That's when you'll know I'm speechless

When the ants no longer want to work
When the wolves wait around and lurk
After the deer has eaten the fallen leaves off the ground
And the ice cream truck no longer makes a sound
That's when you'll know I'm speechless

When I choose to hold my tongue
When I choose no longer to run
After the weight is lifted and I can breathe
When I no longer feel the need not to leave
That's when you'll know I'm speechless

Speechless

Cont'd

I didn't lose my voice, it was a choice
I didn't fail at life or being anyone's trophy wife
I didn't miss out on being happy; just like
I did not miss out on having a pappy
I didn't miss a step as I walked to my own drummer's beat

I became speechless to preserve my sassiness
I became speechless to preserve what I had to say
I became speechless to no one but you
Because what you considered speechless
was the notification that we were through

I became speechless to separate myself from you
You no longer served me and now we are through
Now you're speechless without a clue…
and now I am back to speaking…. Who knew?

Daily Gratitude:

_____

_____

_____

_____

_____

_____.

Pleasure List For Today (Things to Do, Desires & Other Note(s)):

_____

_____

_____

_____

_____

_____.

Today's Affirmation:

_____

_____

_____

_____

_____

_____

_____.

Visualize Your Day:

_____
_____
_____
_____
_____
_____.

Non-Pleasures of Today (Things to Do Tomorrow, Drama(s) of The Day, Possible Failures & Do-Overs):

_____
_____
_____
_____
_____
_____.

Reflections From Today:

_____
_____
_____
_____
_____
_____.

Day 26
Affirmation: I Attract Success

Dream Thinker

Another day to relax and think
But not about pretty little flowers colored pink

I sit and think about me
And how the world is treating thee

A Queen but covered by a mask
A person who can master any task

The world being covered by green grass
People wanting to get to know me, great numbers....in mass

No time for self-doubt
No time to pout

But time to sing
Time for me to get my diamond ring

Time for my king to find me
Time for me to be the Queen I was raised to be

Another moment to remember the past
Catching each minute, not moving too fast

As I sit and think about me
Rising to the calling of what I was meant to be!

Daily Gratitude:

_____

_____

_____

_____

_____

_____ .

Pleasure List For Today (Things to Do, Desires & Other Note(s)):

_____

_____

_____

_____

_____

_____ .

Today's Affirmation:

_____

_____

_____

_____

_____

_____

_____ .

Visualize Your Day:

_____

_____

_____

_____

_____

_____.

Non-Pleasures of Today (Things to Do Tomorrow, Drama(s) of The Day, Possible Failures & Do-Overs):

_____

_____

_____

_____

_____

_____.

Reflections From Today:

_____

_____

_____

_____

_____

_____

_____.

Day 27
Affirmation: I Am Respectful

Calling

Calling you on the phone
And all I get is a dial tone

Calling you back to me
Making it more than it should be

Calling from my mother's house
But you are running away like a stupid little mouse

Calling from the top of my voice
Not realizing that you already made your choice

Calling you another time
At the price of a dime

Calling you and still no one is there
All along you were showing me that you did not care

Calling you like a fool
Going to your house and skipping school

Still calling you and ain't getting nowhere
Calling you and you're still not there

Daily Gratitude:

_____

_____

_____

_____

_____

_____.

Pleasure List For Today (Things to Do, Desires & Other Note(s)):

_____

_____

_____

_____

_____

_____.

Today's Affirmation:

_____

_____

_____

_____

_____

_____

_____.

Visualize Your Day:

_____
_____
_____
_____
_____
_____.

Non-Pleasures of Today (Things to Do Tomorrow, Drama(s) of The Day, Possible Failures & Do-Overs):

_____
_____
_____
_____
_____
_____.

Reflections From Today:

_____
_____
_____
_____
_____
_____.

Day 28
Affirmation: I Am Independent

Where Did You Go?

Nothing has been the same since you've been gone
The radio or computer doesn't stay on as long
I knew that the week would be over soon
Because I was bored by you watching those silly cartoons
What is really going on? I don't really know
You left and said that you would be back
But I haven't been able to see anything but black
The sky is dark grey and the grass is brown
As I sit in this lonely town
Looking up and down, hoping that you come back to me
Because I really don't know where else you could be
And I hated to say "See you later alligator"
But to make me smile and feel better
You replied, "After a while crocodile"
Sadly, my poem is coming to its end
And all of my feelings, tears and smiles have been put in
Can't wait to see you when you arrive
So we can hang out and ride on the tide
But first, where did you go?

Daily Gratitude:

_____

_____

_____

_____

_____

_____.

Pleasure List For Today (Things to Do, Desires & Other Note(s)):

_____

_____

_____

_____

_____

_____.

Today's Affirmation:

_____

_____

_____

_____

_____

_____

_____.

Visualize Your Day:

_____

_____

_____

_____

_____

_____.

Non-Pleasures of Today (Things to Do Tomorrow, Drama(s) of The Day, Possible Failures & Do-Overs):

_____

_____

_____

_____

_____

_____.

Reflections From Today:

_____

_____

_____

_____

_____

_____

_____.

Day 29
Affirmation: I Am Knowledgeable

Sisterhood

What is really going on, I don't know?
How people are beginning to speak
They must think my mind is weak

What is really going on, I don't know?
People are going out of their way to speak
But really don't know what to say
Are we family or are we friends,
Can I depend on you at the end of the day?

What is really going on, I don't know?
What looked like gold, it is no longer hot but cold
Nothing left to shift, turn and mold
The story of a strong sisterhood and bond, left untold

Daily Gratitude:

_____

_____

_____

_____

_____

_____.

Pleasure List For Today (Things to Do, Desires & Other Note(s)):

_____

_____

_____

_____

_____

_____.

Today's Affirmation:

_____

_____

_____

_____

_____

_____

_____.

Visualize Your Day:

_____

_____

_____

_____

_____

_____.

Non-Pleasures of Today (Things to Do Tomorrow, Drama(s) of The Day, Possible Failures & Do-Overs):

_____

_____

_____

_____

_____

_____.

Reflections From Today:

_____

_____

_____

_____

_____

_____

_____.

Day 30
Affirmation: I Am A Creator

Males

Why must these males
Tell these certain tales
About how they need space
And the relationship is moving at a fast pace

What are the feelings that feel so funny
Is it about him having no money?
What are these feelings that we cannot compare
About the love that really was never there

Was it so fake that you could not tell?

Have you not learned the way to tie your ties?
Why must you tell all of these lies?

It is a wonder, how you have no power.
You tried to play a game that you could not win
You made the rules but failed to obey them

The game is now at the end and I must move on to other men
It is now time to make some new rules
Maybe this time you will follow them and not loose

Daily Gratitude:

_____

_____

_____

_____

_____

_____.

Pleasure List For Today (Things to Do, Desires & Other Note(s)):

_____

_____

_____

_____

_____.

Today's Affirmation:

_____

_____

_____

_____

_____

_____.

Visualize Your Day:

_____

_____

_____

_____

_____

_____.

Non-Pleasures of Today (Things to Do Tomorrow, Drama(s) of The Day, Possible Failures & Do-Overs):

_____

_____

_____

_____

_____

_____.

Reflections From Today:

_____

_____

_____

_____

_____

_____

_____.

Day 31
Affirmation: I Am Different

Keisha's Love

Keisha's love is like no one else's love
Sweet but sexy; pretty as a dove

Keisha's love is like one's mother
Quite but active, keeping you captive

Keisha's love is smooth and rich
It can never be forgotten but it is not always around

Keisha's love is calm and nice
Warms the blood, not cold like ice

Keisha's love comes in small pieces,
Not easily mishandled and knows no hate
And always get callbacks for a second date

Keisha's love is forever and ever
And does not tend to forget, no never

Keisha's love only comes around once
If you destroy or misuse it, my love will never let you forget it

Keisha's love is addictive
It should never be mistaken for another's

Daily Gratitude:

_____

_____

_____

_____

_____

_____.

Pleasure List For Today (Things to Do, Desires & Other Note(s)):

_____

_____

_____

_____

_____

_____.

Today's Affirmation:

_____

_____

_____

_____

_____

_____

_____

_____.

Visualize Your Day:

_____
_____
_____
_____
_____
_____.

Non-Pleasures of Today (Things to Do Tomorrow, Drama(s) of The Day, Possible Failures & Do-Overs):

_____
_____
_____
_____
_____
_____.

Reflections From Today:

_____
_____
_____
_____
_____
_____
_____
_____.

Day 32
Affirmation: I Am Focused

My First Love

My first love was not who I had sex with,
Neither did I tongue him down.
He was a respectable young man.
The one I took home to mother.
And she accepted him.
He respected me like no other.

Like no other males did.
This is what made me so attracted to him.
This is what had me sprung, other than his cuteness.
And his name was _____.

Of course I wanted to make love to him.
And, my mother said he would make the ideal husband.
I would love to see how our kids would turn out
If I married him…hmmmmm!
Our first baby, a girl, maybe I could name her Kim.

We broke up because of me.
I regretted it every day.
At the time it happened,
I could not handle what was going on
And I wanted to sink to the bottom of the bay.
I felt as though he was invading my space.
He was getting too close
I pushed him away.

My First Love

Cont'd

This was the first male I said
"I love you" to first and meant it.
What a feeling it was!
This was the first male I said,
"I trust you" to first and meant it.

Our love started as friends for three years.
The relationship lasted for three months.
And our goodbye, only three seconds.

I felt I would always have feelings for him
That beautiful creature, maybe I'll call him, Rim.

We talked off and on
We planned to stay friends forever
But never did.

My first love, just a mere memory
Now I date myself as a remedy
As I am my only first true love

Daily Gratitude:

_____

_____

_____

_____

_____

_____

Pleasure List For Today (Things to Do, Desires & Other Note(s)):

_____

_____

_____

_____

_____

_____

Today's Affirmation:

_____

_____

_____

_____

_____

_____

_____

Visualize Your Day:

_____

_____

_____

_____

_____

_____.

Non-Pleasures of Today (Things to Do Tomorrow, Drama(s) of The Day, Possible Failures & Do-Overs):

_____

_____

_____

_____

_____

_____.

Reflections From Today:

_____

_____

_____

_____

_____

_____.

Day 33
Affirmation: I Am Mindful

My Second Love

My second love was my last love
We fucked and walked through the muck
We were in-separatable and our actions unrepeatable
This one, I could not bring home to mother
Instead, I chose to let her focus on the other

The other males who came before him
We'll call this one Tim
I drew no attention to him, my second love....
I kept him for myself; He was everything
Rim was not....
Not the husband type but all the hype
"Thugged out" and dark-skinned
Muscular and beautiful bright eyes
Tight ass and six-pack abs....
MmmmmMmmmmmmmm!

He was absolutely delicious and smelled divine.
Of course I wanted to fuck him too
He was my kind
I dreamed of having his child and naming him Gem
That is what I would call him

My Second Love

Cont'd

A baby boy, a prince made from his mom
A Queen and his father, a King
But we lost our way
Missing what we had back in the day
I pushed him away
I did not want him to stay
As I had to get back to me
And he was no longer helping to please me
True to me
I had loved and lost myself in the process

Two lovers and one soul
Two hearts and one beat
We had no other choice but to give up that seat and ride solo
To get back to me

Our love started out as friends for seven years.
The relationship lasted for seven months
And our goodbye, seven seconds.

Daily Gratitude:

_____
_____
_____
_____
_____
_____.

Pleasure List For Today (Things to Do, Desires & Other Note(s)):

_____
_____
_____
_____
_____
_____.

Today's Affirmation:

_____
_____
_____
_____
_____
_____.

Visualize Your Day:

_____

_____

_____

_____

_____

_____.

Non-Pleasures of Today (Things to Do Tomorrow, Drama(s) of The Day, Possible Failures & Do-Overs):

_____

_____

_____

_____

_____

_____.

Reflections From Today:

_____

_____

_____

_____

_____

_____.

Day 34
Affirmation: I Am Joyous

To Survive

What is it to say
That this is the American way
To have a job, a house, a car
To go to law school and pass the bar

Going to school and saying it's cool
Not to smoke but learning to use a tool

Who is to say what it is right
Not to stand up and fight
For what is right

Maybe that is not the way?

Maybe I can't learn all that I want to say from a book
Maybe my destiny is to help a crook
Maybe all that I had was took
And now all I can do is look

Then again maybe all I need is a glass of wine
To calm down and realize that everything will be fine
Because this world is not only mine
Even though it takes up all of my time

Since the books are not written in my words
Maybe all of that nonsense is for the birds
So, who is it to say that this is the American way?
Me, I am the one who will have the last say

Daily Gratitude:

_____

_____

_____

_____

_____

_____.

Pleasure List For Today (Things to Do, Desires & Other Note(s)):

_____

_____

_____

_____

_____

_____.

Today's Affirmation:

_____

_____

_____

_____

_____

_____.

Visualize Your Day:

_____

_____

_____

_____

_____

_____.

Non-Pleasures of Today (Things to Do Tomorrow, Drama(s) of The Day, Possible Failures & Do-Overs):

_____

_____

_____

_____

_____

_____.

Reflections From Today:

_____

_____

_____

_____

_____

_____

_____.

Day 35
Affirmation: I Am Phenomenal
Inner Youthful Thought

As I sit around and write down my thoughts
I think about my last days in high school
And wonder about what I will be taught

It is a wonder of how things changed suddenly
It is just too fast, feels like things are running me
Thinking about everything, now and then,
But especially about the past

Tears run down my face
As I remember and think about my friends
How the relationships grow
And who will be with me
When I finish the race
Wow!
Everything is truly moving at a fast pace

As I continue to look at my future
What lies before me in this world
I know that I need plenty of nurturing
As I rise and form my beauty as a pearl

Daily Gratitude:

_____
_____
_____
_____
_____
_____.

Pleasure List For Today (Things to Do, Desires & Other Note(s)):

_____
_____
_____
_____
_____
_____.

Today's Affirmation:

_____
_____
_____
_____
_____
_____
_____.

Visualize Your Day:

_____
_____
_____
_____
_____
_____.

Non-Pleasures of Today (Things to Do Tomorrow, Drama(s) of The Day, Possible Failures & Do-Overs):

_____
_____
_____
_____
_____.

Reflections From Today:

_____
_____
_____
_____
_____
_____.

Day 36
Affirmation: I Am Excited

How Good is It

Remembering the night
When we did everything right
No more creeping in the night
No more useless fights

Instead, I am good to you
No more feeling blue
No more feeling that we aren't true
But that you were vibing with me too

How can I explain what I feel
How can a person describe a rose's smell
How can I never tell
That the feelings are real

All that I used to do
With you not having a clue
Never getting back to you
Starting my life brand new

Now that it is so
And now that everyone knows
Us planning to sit your mother on the first row
Of our wedding....

So now, there is no end
Me signing my name with the official pen
No more committing of sins
And no more lying to our kin about.....
How Good It Is

Daily Gratitude:

_____
_____
_____
_____
_____
_____.

Pleasure List For Today (Things to Do, Desires & Other Note(s)):

_____
_____
_____
_____
_____
_____.

Today's Affirmation:

_____
_____
_____
_____
_____
_____
_____.

Visualize Your Day:

_____

_____

_____

_____

_____

_____.

Non-Pleasures of Today (Things to Do Tomorrow, Drama(s) of The Day, Possible Failures & Do-Overs):

_____

_____

_____

_____

_____

_____.

Reflections From Today:

_____

_____

_____

_____

_____

_____

_____.

Day 37
Affirmation: I Am Persistent

This Place Today

Today would have been a good day
If it was the last day in May
I thought of stuff all today
Waiting for a call, just to say hey

Just lying around thinking about today
How people act in many different ways
All the words written for demonstration
But never spoken in a conversation

One for one and two for two
Feeling that nothing could take the place of you
Not wanting to grow apart
But what else to do when we don't speak from the heart

What are the reasons for all of the lies
That you tell from time to time
Thinking when I am old, I'll read this through
And see that others were feeling this way too

For the end is now here
And, I wrote all of these words with lots of care
When I am much older, I will read back through these pages
And see how much I have been through

This Place Today
Cont'd

One for one and two for two
These words can never show how much I loved you
Who are these people or person I'm talking about?
It's the world in general, not to point anyone out

When we part and meet back up, we will have a lot to talk about
Especially those things we kept buried deep down inside our heart
This place I am at today
Only shows that I really do mean what I say
I loved you too in response to you

Daily Gratitude:

_____
_____
_____
_____
_____
_____.

Pleasure List For Today (Things to Do, Desires & Other Note(s)):

_____
_____
_____
_____
_____.

Today's Affirmation:

_____
_____
_____
_____
_____
_____
_____.

Visualize Your Day:

_____

_____

_____

_____

_____

_____.

Non-Pleasures of Today (Things to Do Tomorrow, Drama(s) of The Day, Possible Failures & Do-Overs):

_____

_____

_____

_____

_____

_____.

Reflections From Today:

_____

_____

_____

_____

_____

_____.

Day 38
Affirmation: Today, I Will Express Myself & Live In My Truth

Tired, Numb And Dumb

It's a process you go through.
First, you're tired of the stupid shit
The arguments, the watching and waking up
Throughout the night
The stupid shit and all-day fights
Anyone in their right mind would get tired of that dumb shit

Next after the fight, into the late night,
Is a numbing feeling of
Why am I still here?
Why can't I already be there?
The numbing won't let you shed a tear
Instead, you stay up late at night sitting in a chair
Eyes open, heart closed, autopilot on, and numb

Last is the dumb effect
After you've taken the shit off of someone else
Sitting and thinking about no one but yourself
Debating the choice, right or wrong
Debating your steps….wondering, Am I dumb?

It's the effects of being tired….numb….and dumb
It's after your gut told you to get up and leave
It's after you told yourself there's no longer any truth to believe

Daily Gratitude:

_____

_____

_____

_____

_____

_____.

Pleasure List For Today (Things to Do, Desires & Other Note(s)):

_____

_____

_____

_____

_____

_____.

Today's Affirmation:

_____

_____

_____

_____

_____

_____.

Visualize Your Day:

_____
_____
_____
_____
_____
_____ .

Non-Pleasures of Today (Things to Do Tomorrow, Drama(s) of The Day, Possible Failures & Do-Overs):

_____
_____
_____
_____
_____
_____ .

Reflections From Today:

_____
_____
_____
_____
_____
_____ .

Day 39
Affirmation: I Am Energetic

I Love You

Words can't express exactly how someone
Falls into the hands of another
But the feelings do show and the two would know

Words can't express exactly how a person
Feels when the other person is around
But feelings can show with phone calls,
Long conversations, sexy tones
And feelings not held inside

Words can't express exactly how I think when
Wanting to stop you in the middle of the sentences
To say what I feel
Wanting to see you right at that moment in time

Yet, afraid to say it, don't know how you will respond
Don't choose to make it any more than needed
No more attention to be created

Afraid to tell you
These three words that are so powerful
Afraid of your response
Afraid to say I love you

If it is true, I will say it to you
But for now, I will withhold my feelings

Words can't express
But feelings can show that I truly do love you

Daily Gratitude:

_____

_____

_____

_____

_____

_____.

Pleasure List For Today (Things to Do, Desires & Other Note(s)):

_____

_____

_____

_____

_____

_____.

Today's Affirmation:

_____

_____

_____

_____

_____

_____

_____.

Visualize Your Day:

_____

_____

_____

_____

_____

_____.

Non-Pleasures of Today (Things to Do Tomorrow, Drama(s) of The Day, Possible Failures & Do-Overs):

_____

_____

_____

_____

_____

_____.

Reflections From Today:

_____

_____

_____

_____

_____

_____

_____.

Day 40
Affirmation: I Am Light

My First Time

I am scared of the feelings you give me
The feelings come too fast
Nervous of what I am getting myself into

Does he mean what he says?
Will I regret it?
Why should I?
Everything he does, I love

Do my feelings show what I feel?
What do I want to say?
How do I want to say it?
Will sex help?

The exchange of our feelings, our emotions, our souls
Feeling you inside of me
You being a part of me
My First

The first male I will feel inside of me
Will this happen?
Do I want this to happen?
Will this show my love for you?
What will it take?
Have I already shown my love?

Words can't express but my actions will show.
What I feel….
After my first time

Daily Gratitude:

_____

_____

_____

_____

_____

_____.

Pleasure List For Today (Things to Do, Desires & Other Note(s)):

_____

_____

_____

_____

_____

_____.

Today's Affirmation:

_____

_____

_____

_____

_____

_____

_____.

Visualize Your Day:

_____
_____
_____
_____
_____
_____ .

Non-Pleasures of Today (Things to Do Tomorrow, Drama(s) of The Day, Possible Failures & Do-Overs):

_____
_____
_____
_____
_____
_____ .

Reflections From Today:

_____
_____
_____
_____
_____
_____ .

Day 41
Affirmation: I Am Understanding

Hell's Depth Can Be Endless

You will rot in hell
For what you say today
To your mother, sister and people around the way

You are covered with burdens
With one on top of your head
They run through your mind day and night
And, you still don't see that everyone's blood is the color red

When you say you're ready to go….
I wonder what is keeping you
When you say you are ready to move on….
I wonder who is that who keeps beeping you
Playa, Playa, is who you think you are
But in my story, you are no longer the star

Down you go
Close the curtains
There's no more to this show

And for your last script
When you say your last verse
Tell me, how is it living in hell
And living in adverse

Daily Gratitude:

_____

_____

_____

_____

_____

_____.

Pleasure List For Today (Things to Do, Desires & Other Note(s)):

_____

_____

_____

_____

_____

_____.

Today's Affirmation:

_____

_____

_____

_____

_____

_____

_____.

Visualize Your Day:

_____
_____
_____
_____
_____
_____.

Non-Pleasures of Today (Things to Do Tomorrow, Drama(s) of The Day, Possible Failures & Do-Overs):

_____
_____
_____
_____
_____
_____.

Reflections From Today:

_____
_____
_____
_____
_____
_____
_____.

Day 42
Affirmation: I Am Enthusiastic

Being Just Me

I thought you were all I wanted, all I needed, all my answers
I thought I was all you dreamed of, all you cared about, all you longed for
Being just me as happy as can be, I hid my pain in the rain
I shared my thoughts but only in my brain.

Not knowing the hurt,
Not wanting the feelings of sadness, loneliness and isolation
Until I met the real me, the one I truly needed,
The only one I truly wanted, the one with all the answers
The only one who showed me what being just me was all about

Now I am able to stand up and shout,
To tell the world what I am all about
And to follow my heart, I once was stupid but now I am being smart
Being just me as happy as I can be with my new self
Being just me, which is all that I can be

Daily Gratitude:

_____

_____

_____

_____

_____

_____.

Pleasure List For Today (Things to Do, Desires & Other Note(s)):

_____

_____

_____

_____

_____

_____.

Today's Affirmation:

_____

_____

_____

_____

_____

_____

_____.

Visualize Your Day:

_____

_____

_____

_____

_____

_____.

Non-Pleasures of Today (Things to Do Tomorrow, Drama(s) of The Day, Possible Failures & Do-Overs):

_____

_____

_____

_____

_____

_____.

Reflections From Today:

_____

_____

_____

_____

_____

_____

_____.

Day 43
Affirmation: I Am Energy

It's All Over Now

When two people know each other
And see them day after day
They are supposed to meet and greet each other
But you can tell that things have changed
Because we don't even speak anymore

When we first met I could not wait
To feel that sensation …but what happened
To the words in our first conversation
Just getting to know each other and exchanging information

Reminders of the other night and of all the temptations
We talked it over
And we didn't want to add someone new to the population
We never said I love you but we knew it was true
You told me how the other girls could not compare to me and you

So what did it all mean
Was it just a long dream
In the summertime, our personal time
We have nothing to show
For the love that we did not get to know

Daily Gratitude:

_____

_____

_____

_____

_____

_____.

Pleasure List For Today (Things to Do, Desires & Other Note(s)):

_____

_____

_____

_____

_____.

Today's Affirmation:

_____

_____

_____

_____

_____

_____.

Visualize Your Day:

_____

_____

_____

_____

_____

_____.

Non-Pleasures of Today (Things to Do Tomorrow, Drama(s) of The Day, Possible Failures & Do-Overs):

_____

_____

_____

_____

_____

_____.

Reflections From Today:

_____

_____

_____

_____

_____

_____

_____.

Day 44
Affirmation: I Am Brillant

Where I Want To Be

Sitting out in the warm sun
As I suck on my fingers after eating a honey bun

Waiting to be wrapped in your arms as you hold me tight
Thinking about the days when we did not fight

Feeling the cold drops of sweat running down my back
Not regretting the days I took you back

As your eyes tend to wander
I do not sit back and ponder

Because he is at home with me
Just where he said he would be

Waking up in the morning, smelling eggs with cheese
You asking for some ass, begging and saying please

As the sun goes down, so do we
Being as happy as can be

Because you are still at peace with me
And this is the place where I want to be

Daily Gratitude:

_____

_____

_____

_____

_____

_____.

Pleasure List For Today (Things to Do, Desires & Other Note(s)):

_____

_____

_____

_____

_____

_____.

Today's Affirmation:

_____

_____

_____

_____

_____

_____.

Visualize Your Day:

_____
_____
_____
_____
_____
_____.

Non-Pleasures of Today (Things to Do Tomorrow, Drama(s) of The Day, Possible Failures & Do-Overs):

_____
_____
_____
_____
_____
_____.

Reflections From Today:

_____
_____
_____
_____
_____
_____

Day 45
Affirmation: I Am Full Of Potential

Gotta Go

I try not to speak because it won't differ
The way we look, it seems so bitter

Next to you, I feel sad and blue
Next to me, I was making you all that you could be

You rejected me and all that I would say
You acted like you didn't see me, didn't offer an umbrella on a rainy day

No more wondering while looking out of the window
No more feelings for us to rekindle

Decided to stop trying to make things work
Because I was the one that ended up hurt

I talk with the Lord to give me peace
So that the pain you cause would soon come to a cease

Can a man's words destroy the soul?
Can a woman's words make you whole?

I need to live again and find someone new
Because anything else except you would do

Daily Gratitude:

_____

_____

_____

_____

_____

_____.

Pleasure List For Today (Things to Do, Desires & Other Note(s)):

_____

_____

_____

_____

_____.

Today's Affirmation:

_____

_____

_____

_____

_____

_____.

Visualize Your Day:

_____

_____

_____

_____

_____

_____.

Non-Pleasures of Today (Things to Do Tomorrow, Drama(s) of The Day, Possible Failures & Do-Overs):

_____

_____

_____

_____

_____

_____.

Reflections From Today:

_____

_____

_____

_____

_____

_____

_____.

Day 46
Affirmation: I Am Forgiven

Something Like That....

I guess you can still find true love
But not at the front door

Maybe a message by mouth from a white dove
Or by one letter, two, many more

Not from beauty will you find him
But from intelligence that will guide you

Maybe not a Mark, Tony or Jim
But definitely someone above the rim

And when love is found,
Maybe falling out of the window and up to the sky
With feeling the feel of a natural high

Open your eyes wider because it is out there
Love waiting for someone like you who care

Daily Gratitude:

_____

_____

_____

_____

_____

_____

Pleasure List For Today (Things to Do, Desires & Other Note(s)):

_____

_____

_____

_____

_____

Today's Affirmation:

_____

_____

_____

_____

_____

_____

Visualize Your Day:

_____

_____

_____

_____

_____

_____ .

Non-Pleasures of Today (Things to Do Tomorrow, Drama(s) of The Day, Possible Failures & Do-Overs):

_____

_____

_____

_____

_____ .

Reflections From Today:

_____

_____

_____

_____

_____

_____ .

Day 47
Affirmation: I Am Thoughtful

My Soul Brothers

He sits and talks on the phone
To someone who is unknown

About the things happening in this house
Nothing but negativity coming from his mouth

Telling others what we do
Not once mentioning that he was wrong too

It is so sad to see him there
Make me mad, don't even want to be here

Talking with no sense
Acting like he's all tense

How funny it is
Him wanting to do harm but can't hurt a fly

As he sits and talks on the phone
Making sure to maintain a low tone

I can no longer hear, I can no longer tell
What is being said or if he's keeping it real

Oh, brother!

Daily Gratitude:

_____
_____
_____
_____
_____
_____.

Pleasure List For Today (Things to Do, Desires & Other Note(s)):

_____
_____
_____
_____
_____
_____.

Today's Affirmation:

_____
_____
_____
_____
_____
_____
_____.

Visualize Your Day:

_____

_____

_____

_____

_____

_____.

Non-Pleasures of Today (Things to Do Tomorrow, Drama(s) of The Day, Possible Failures & Do-Overs):

_____

_____

_____

_____

_____

_____.

Reflections From Today:

_____

_____

_____

_____

_____

_____

_____.

Day 48
Affirmation: I Am Glowing

Faces

All the faces I see today
All of them having something to say

The way their lips are big and small
And some of them only a height of five feet tall

Pretty dark skin that hides in the night
With the same dark-colored eyes that make everything feel right

Braided hair with bows on the end
Remembering back when I was ten

Pretty white teeth with a smile from ear to ear
Never holding back, not even a salty little tear

All the faces I see today
All say the same thing but in a different way

Daily Gratitude:

_____

_____

_____

_____

_____

_____.

Pleasure List For Today (Things to Do, Desires & Other Note(s)):

_____

_____

_____

_____

_____

_____.

Today's Affirmation:

_____

_____

_____

_____

_____

_____

_____.

Visualize Your Day:

_____

_____

_____

_____

_____

_____.

Non-Pleasures of Today (Things to Do Tomorrow, Drama(s) of The Day, Possible Failures & Do-Overs):

_____

_____

_____

_____

_____

_____.

Reflections From Today:

_____

_____

_____

_____

_____

_____

_____

Day 49
Affirmation: I Feel Good

Tick, Tock, Tick

Time is passing and so are we
We can't just sit around sipping on tea

Gotta get out and do something
Won't spend any more time crying

Gotta get out and do something
Cause on the inside I feel like I'm dying

For me, opportunities come and go
As for you, no one really knows

Time to move on, so get on with your day
I no longer have the time to count the sun's rays

Our moments were nice and so were you
No more about me, what are you going to do?

Can't hold me back, no turning around
My bags are packed and I'm moving to higher ground

Time is passing and so am I
Reaching out my hand and heart to get a piece of that lovable pie

Daily Gratitude:

_____
_____
_____
_____
_____
_____.

Pleasure List For Today (Things to Do, Desires & Other Note(s)):

_____
_____
_____
_____
_____.

Today's Affirmation:

_____
_____
_____
_____
_____
_____
_____.

Visualize Your Day:

_____

_____

_____

_____

_____

_____.

Non-Pleasures of Today (Things to Do Tomorrow, Drama(s) of The Day, Possible Failures & Do-Overs):

_____

_____

_____

_____

_____

_____.

Reflections From Today:

_____

_____

_____

_____

_____

_____

_____.

Day 50
Affirmation: I Am Flexible

Cold

This world that is my life
Has me on needles and pins
Being watchful of the knife
With reoccurring hope that does not end

Gotta get away
And move on to a different beat
Hoping to see a beautiful day
Where there is no dead corn to eat

In the fields, the birds do sing
In the forest, the trees are still green
On my finger, there aren't any rings
Because this life is so mean

Nothing to eat
No house to live in
No shoes on my feet
Having only the Lord as a kin

I can only depend on me
With no help from them
Loving with nothing that is free
All I can do is believe in me

Daily Gratitude:

_____

_____

_____

_____

_____

_____.

Pleasure List For Today (Things to Do, Desires & Other Note(s)):

_____

_____

_____

_____

_____

_____.

Today's Affirmation:

_____

_____

_____

_____

_____

_____.

Visualize Your Day:

_____

_____

_____

_____

_____

_____.

Non-Pleasures of Today (Things to Do Tomorrow, Drama(s) of The Day, Possible Failures & Do-Overs):

_____

_____

_____

_____

_____

_____.

Reflections From Today:

_____

_____

_____

_____

_____

_____

Day 51
Affirmation: I Am An Overcomer

Our First Meeting

Before we met
We would meet and greet
But things have changed
Now, we don't even speak

At first, we laughed and had lots of conversation
But now there is nothing to say
No more interesting information

Never saying I love you but knowing the feelings were true
You telling me how nothing else could compare to us, just me and you

So what did it all mean, was it all a long dream
Because after our last meeting
We were no longer working like a team

Daily Gratitude:

_____
_____
_____
_____
_____
_____.

Pleasure List For Today (Things to Do, Desires & Other Note(s)):

_____
_____
_____
_____
_____.

Today's Affirmation:

_____
_____
_____
_____
_____
_____
_____.

Visualize Your Day:

_____
_____
_____
_____
_____
_____.

Non-Pleasures of Today (Things to Do Tomorrow, Drama(s) of The Day, Possible Failures & Do-Overs):

_____
_____
_____
_____
_____
_____.

Reflections From Today:

_____
_____
_____
_____
_____
_____
_____.

Day 52
Affirmation: I Am An Efficient Learner

Funny

Simple questions I ask myself
Of why I take the time out
To listen to the bullshit on the phone
Day after day, round and about

Memories of the first time
Funny times of reuniting
Made me happy because I thought
That you were really mine

The past is the past
The present contains the now
Thinking about your dumb ass
The times we traveled away from this town

There's nothing else to say but goodbye
Maybe we'll meet another time
Because right now it seems so funny
How you say that I only want you for your money

Daily Gratitude:

_____

_____

_____

_____

_____

_____.

Pleasure List For Today (Things to Do, Desires & Other Note(s)):

_____

_____

_____

_____

_____

_____.

Today's Affirmation:

_____

_____

_____

_____

_____

_____

_____.

Visualize Your Day:

_____
_____
_____
_____
_____
_____.

Non-Pleasures of Today (Things to Do Tomorrow, Drama(s) of The Day, Possible Failures & Do-Overs):

_____
_____
_____
_____
_____
_____.

Reflections From Today:

_____
_____
_____
_____
_____
_____
_____.

Day 53
Affirmation: I Will Persevere

Valentine's Day

I'll see how much you really care
When I don't get a card
Or any chocolates to share

I'll see how much you really care
When I am lying by your side
When you don't turn my way to see if I am still alive

I'll see how much you really care
We I ask for you
And you're not there

I'll see how much you really care
When I pour my gifts into you
And all you do is give me a glimpse
Not even a stare

Daily Gratitude:

_____

_____

_____

_____

_____

_____.

Pleasure List For Today (Things to Do, Desires & Other Note(s)):

_____

_____

_____

_____

_____

_____.

Today's Affirmation:

_____

_____

_____

_____

_____

_____.

Visualize Your Day:

_____

_____

_____

_____

_____

_____.

Non-Pleasures of Today (Things to Do Tomorrow, Drama(s) of The Day, Possible Failures & Do-Overs):

_____

_____

_____

_____

_____

_____.

Reflections From Today:

_____

_____

_____

_____

_____

_____.

Day 54
Affirmation: I Am Stress-Free

Loving You

Not spending too much time together
But knowing that we rather
Be close and hold hands
Me telling you that you're the only man
For me, no one else can do
Not picturing myself with anyone else but you
Thinking about you, wanting you near
Me feeling secure with nothing to fear
Because I know that we have trust
And that this relationship was a must
As we grow with each other
Having our children
Me being called their mother
The feeling feels so good like I knew it would
Me doing what I do, Which is only loving you

Daily Gratitude:

_____

_____

_____

_____

_____

_____.

Pleasure List For Today (Things to Do, Desires & Other Note(s)):

_____

_____

_____

_____

_____

_____.

Today's Affirmation:

_____

_____

_____

_____

_____

_____

_____.

Visualize Your Day:

_____

_____

_____

_____

_____

_____.

Non-Pleasures of Today (Things to Do Tomorrow, Drama(s) of The Day, Possible Failures & Do-Overs):

_____

_____

_____

_____

_____

_____.

Reflections From Today:

_____

_____

_____

_____

_____

_____

Day 55
Affirmation: I Am Exceptional

Happy

Sitting here in the shade; drinking my tall cool glass of lemonade
Wondering about what happened to us,
Thinking our being together was a must

Not knowing what we were truly about;
Always ending the night with a fight and a shout

As I sit back against the tree;
Knowing that you would never find someone else as good as me

I think again about the two of us and thought… damn,
Where was the trust?

You were following me, and I was questioning you
I ain't got time for this mess, both of us being a pest
Sitting here in the shade; drinking my tall cool glass of lemonade

I turn around only to see a reflection of me and only me
Alone but happy, which is the only way to be

Daily Gratitude:

_____

_____

_____

_____

_____

_____.

Pleasure List For Today (Things to Do, Desires & Other Note(s)):

_____

_____

_____

_____

_____.

Today's Affirmation:

_____

_____

_____

_____

_____

_____.

Visualize Your Day:

_____

_____

_____

_____

_____

_____.

Non-Pleasures of Today (Things to Do Tomorrow, Drama(s) of The Day, Possible Failures & Do-Overs):

_____

_____

_____

_____

_____

_____.

Reflections From Today:

_____

_____

_____

_____

_____

_____

_____.

Day 56
Affirmation: I Am Worthy

Dedication

Every day I lay down dreaming
But wake up screaming

Trying to give you another chance
But still knowing that I need to advance

Continuing to say that you will be faithful
Continuing to make love for other reasons besides being faithful

Looking in the mirror with me in my thongs
Singing every word from our favorite love songs

Moving on from here for no reason to stay
No use in waiting for the rain to melt away memories of clay

Daily Gratitude:

_____

_____

_____

_____

_____

_____.

Pleasure List For Today (Things to Do, Desires & Other Note(s)):

_____

_____

_____

_____

_____

_____.

Today's Affirmation:

_____

_____

_____

_____

_____

_____

_____.

Visualize Your Day:

_____

_____

_____

_____

_____

_____ .

Non-Pleasures of Today (Things to Do Tomorrow, Drama(s) of The Day, Possible Failures & Do-Overs):

_____

_____

_____

_____

_____

_____ .

Reflections From Today:

_____

_____

_____

_____

_____

_____

_____

_____ .

Day 57

Affirmation: I Deserve The Best

Hell Hole

You might just rot in hell
For what you will say

To your friends and family
People around the way

You are covered with burdens
From the top of your head

It runs through your mind day and night
Not realizing that your blood is still red

You say that you're ready to go, then leave
You say you are ready to die, then do it

How shameful it is, how unreal?
Not knowing that you are already living in hell

Daily Gratitude:

_____
_____
_____
_____
_____
_____.

Pleasure List For Today (Things to Do, Desires & Other Note(s)):

_____
_____
_____
_____
_____
_____.

Today's Affirmation:

_____
_____
_____
_____
_____
_____.

Visualize Your Day:

_____

_____

_____

_____

_____

_____.

Non-Pleasures of Today (Things to Do Tomorrow, Drama(s) of The Day, Possible Failures & Do-Overs):

_____

_____

_____

_____

_____

_____.

Reflections From Today:

_____

_____

_____

_____

_____

_____

_____.

Day 58
Affirmation: I Am Calm

Ain't Always Pleasure

It ain't none of their business is what I heard from your mouth
But when I came home and saw the two of you,
All I could say was get out
Nothing was important anymore,
Especially since you weren't going to walk through my door
I thought that maybe by this time, it would be you and me
But I guess I was wrong so I'll just let it be

I see now there's a new girl in your life
Did you know how her last boyfriend died by the knife?
Not by a stranger or in a street fight
No, it was your new girl, the one you sleep beside at night

So I found no use to tell you twice
Because then you would think that I wasn't acting nice
Maybe it was their business of what went on that night
Just think, if I had known, things could have turned out alright

But now I am here between these four walls
Just waiting to make three more phone calls
To prove that I did no wrong
Even if I did know that she carried a blade in her thong
I tried to see the best for us and to keep you away from the harm
But you couldn't let it be, saying that you needed to be free
So now you lay, motionless your grave
Surrounded by dirt, dark as a cave

Ain't Always Pleasure

Cont'd

For me, I'm no longer in a cell
Was I her accomplice? Hell no, that's why I made bail
Decided to stay quiet, no one to trust, no one to tell
Happy once again, living only with me
No more attachments and happy to say
That I am the one finally free

Daily Gratitude:

_____

_____

_____

_____

_____

_____.

Pleasure List For Today (Things to Do, Desires & Other Note(s)):

_____

_____

_____

_____

_____

_____.

Today's Affirmation:

_____

_____

_____

_____

_____

_____

_____.

Visualize Your Day:

_____

_____

_____

_____

_____

_____.

Non-Pleasures of Today (Things to Do Tomorrow, Drama(s) of The Day, Possible Failures & Do-Overs):

_____

_____

_____

_____

_____.

Reflections From Today:

_____

_____

_____

_____

_____

_____.

Day 59
Affirmation: I Am Wise

Inbox News

It's like realizing that your fingernails do grow
And that it is not for you to know
He was not out there doing work
But sleeping with everyone including the clerk

Oh how funny it seems to be
When it is all happening to me
So now all I can do is shout
Don't touch me, get the hell out

Wondering why am I here
Shedding of these undeserving tears
Over a silly piece of shit like you
Not knowing what else to do

Hurting all over, not just from the heart
Going to pick myself up and do something smart
Leave your black ass and don't return
Because I can no longer stand the burn

Daily Gratitude:

_____

_____

_____

_____

_____

_____.

Pleasure List For Today (Things to Do, Desires & Other Note(s)):

_____

_____

_____

_____

_____

_____.

Today's Affirmation:

_____

_____

_____

_____

_____

_____

_____.

Visualize Your Day:

_____

_____

_____

_____

_____

_____.

Non-Pleasures of Today (Things to Do Tomorrow, Drama(s) of The Day, Possible Failures & Do-Overs):

_____

_____

_____

_____

_____

_____.

Reflections From Today:

_____

_____

_____

_____

_____

_____

_____.

Day 60
Affirmation: I Am Powerful

Ms. Lady Bug

They call me, Ms. Lady Bug, as I sit in my thinking chair
Letting my fingers run through my hair

Wondering and pondering about the past
The days you did not mind kissing my ass

Now another day has arrived
And all you do is sit and think of beehives

I call for you to come and see me
And when you never answered, I just let it be

I figured that you did not have a good reason
For why you did not call for a month, a whole season

…and I ponder, Why is it that you are still not here
Just like in the past, you were never really near

I, Ms. Lady Bug, still sitting in my thinking chair
And letting my fingers run through my hair

I thought about it once more and now I see
That we really were not meant to be

Daily Gratitude:

_____

_____

_____

_____

_____

_____ .

Pleasure List For Today (Things to Do, Desires & Other Note(s)):

_____

_____

_____

_____

_____

_____ .

Today's Affirmation:

_____

_____

_____

_____

_____

_____

_____ .

Visualize Your Day:

_____

_____

_____

_____

_____

_____.

Non-Pleasures of Today (Things to Do Tomorrow, Drama(s) of The Day, Possible Failures & Do-Overs):

_____

_____

_____

_____

_____

_____.

Reflections From Today:

_____

_____

_____

_____

_____

_____.

Day 61
Affirmation: I Can Accomplish Anything

Never Fails

Every time I let myself go
It seems like you already know
What to say and do
For me to take back what I said about you

Every time I come back, back home to see you
It seems like you always know
What to say or do
For me to say that I don't love you

Every single time I call, write and wait for the reply
It seems like you already know
What to say or do
So that I know I won't be hearing back from you

Every time you asked I gave
I knew that you would find a way
You would know what to say or do
So that I could regret those words too

Every time I spoke of you and claimed that we were true
I was not surprised by what you knew
What to say or do
To make my friends not like you

Every time you came to the house
Early or late, I let you in
And still you knew what to say or do
For me to say, "Don't return because we're thru"

Daily Gratitude:

_____

_____

_____

_____

_____

_____.

Pleasure List For Today (Things to Do, Desires & Other Note(s)):

_____

_____

_____

_____

_____

_____.

Today's Affirmation:

_____

_____

_____

_____

_____

_____

_____.

Visualize Your Day:

_____

_____

_____

_____

_____

_____.

Non-Pleasures of Today (Things to Do Tomorrow, Drama(s) of The Day, Possible Failures & Do-Overs):

_____

_____

_____

_____

_____

_____.

Reflections From Today:

_____

_____

_____

_____

_____

_____

_____.

Day 62
Affirmation: I Am An Achiever

To Look And Notice

Only when you look at me I know that you care
And when I look at you, you know that I will be near

Only when you look at me I know that it is your love appeal
And when I speak to you, you know that it is real

Only when you smile I know that it is peaceful, not blue
And when I touch you, you will know that it is true

I tried to live, breathe and go on without you
But it only got harder to think, work and live without you

Everyone sounds like they're calling your name
Nothing feels the same

Only when you hold me I know that it is forever
And when I say it, you'll know we'll always be together

Daily Gratitude:

_____

_____

_____

_____

_____

_____ .

Pleasure List For Today (Things to Do, Desires & Other Note(s)):

_____

_____

_____

_____

_____

_____ .

Today's Affirmation:

_____

_____

_____

_____

_____

_____

_____ .

Visualize Your Day:

_____

_____

_____

_____

_____

_____.

Non-Pleasures of Today (Things to Do Tomorrow, Drama(s) of The Day, Possible Failures & Do-Overs):

_____

_____

_____

_____

_____

_____.

Reflections From Today:

_____

_____

_____

_____

_____

_____

_____.

Day 63
Affirmation: I Am Diplomatic

Only You

Lord, you were always there
Whenever I called
Lord, you will always be here
Even as I shop in the mall
Only you can love and not count my wrongs
Only you can show me that it's my decision
How I decide to show up all year long
Lord, continue to work in me
Please just don't let me be
Lord, help me to change my ways as I try to do as you say
Because only you can judge me on that last judgment day

Amen

Daily Gratitude:

_____

_____

_____

_____

_____

_____ .

Pleasure List For Today (Things to Do, Desires & Other Note(s)):

_____

_____

_____

_____

_____

_____ .

Today's Affirmation:

_____

_____

_____

_____

_____

_____

_____ .

Visualize Your Day:

_____

_____

_____

_____

_____

_____.

**Non-Pleasures of Today (Things to Do Tomorrow, Drama(s) of
The Day, Possible Failures & Do-Overs):**

_____

_____

_____

_____

_____

_____.

Reflections From Today:

_____

_____

_____

_____

_____

_____

_____.

Day 64
Affirmation: I Am Wealthy

Sounds Nice

I got a good man
Who doesn't mind taking a stand

With me or for me
He understands

Him trying with all his might
Us not getting into any fights

Because he never has to go through withdrawal from me
Me not knowing how addictive I could be

This time, my relationship will last
Forgetting and forgiving things that happened in the past

Because I got a good man
And I'm grateful as this was always a part of my life's plan

Daily Gratitude:

_____
_____
_____
_____
_____
_____

Pleasure List For Today (Things to Do, Desires & Other Note(s)):

_____
_____
_____
_____
_____

Today's Affirmation:

_____
_____
_____
_____
_____
_____
_____

Visualize Your Day:

_____

_____

_____

_____

_____

_____.

Non-Pleasures of Today (Things to Do Tomorrow, Drama(s) of The Day, Possible Failures & Do-Overs):

_____

_____

_____

_____

_____

_____.

Reflections From Today:

_____

_____

_____

_____

_____

_____

_____.

Day 65
Affirmation: I Am Grateful

Little Miss

Little Miss Buttercup looking as sexy as can be
Little Miss Buttercup, who is she?

The one with the chocolate brown face
The one who tends to walk at her own pace

Not trying to impress those she doesn't like
Not trying to buy herself a man called Mike

Instead, she is happy with herself, no need to think twice
Because everything about Little Miss Buttercup is nice

Little Miss Buttercup looking as sexy as can be
Little Miss Buttercup, who is she?

Oh, she is the one holding the delicious-tasting cup of tea
Little Miss Buttercup is no one other than me!

Daily Gratitude:

_____

_____

_____

_____

_____

_____

Pleasure List For Today (Things to Do, Desires & Other Note(s)):

_____

_____

_____

_____

_____

_____

Today's Affirmation:

_____

_____

_____

_____

_____

_____

_____

Visualize Your Day:

_____
_____
_____
_____
_____
_____.

Non-Pleasures of Today (Things to Do Tomorrow, Drama(s) of The Day, Possible Failures & Do-Overs):

_____
_____
_____
_____
_____.

Reflections From Today:

_____
_____
_____
_____
_____
_____
_____.

Day 66
Affirmation: I Am Compassionate

Monday Nights

Coming over to the house
Sneaking to my bedroom as soft as a mouse
Under the covers, then on top of me
Me waiting for you to fulfill my every fantasy

Thrusting inside of me, moving it deeper in
Me feeling like I am lying on stick pins
Legs being forced into the air
Then you pulling on my hair

Not yet calling your name
But praying that one day, you will be tamed
You all over me, like the wilderness, can't handle the rush
Breathing so hard with every word I must….
…..Stop and ask for forgiveness cause this feels like a sin

But it is also so hot, so wet, so nice
Me desiring a piece of ice
And Lord knows that I should be asleep
No one hearing a peep

But you're already inside
So I tell you to keep going all while knowing
That if my mother sees me like this
All I am going to feel is her fist

But it feels so damn fucking good!
Those good ole Monday nights
Being with you made everything seem right!

Daily Gratitude:

_____
_____
_____
_____
_____
_____.

Pleasure List For Today (Things to Do, Desires & Other Note(s)):

_____
_____
_____
_____
_____
_____.

Today's Affirmation:

_____
_____
_____
_____
_____
_____.

Visualize Your Day:

_____
_____
_____
_____
_____
_____.

Non-Pleasures of Today (Things to Do Tomorrow, Drama(s) of The Day, Possible Failures & Do-Overs):

_____
_____
_____
_____
_____
_____.

Reflections From Today:

_____
_____
_____
_____
_____
_____
_____.

Day 67
Affirmation: I Am Loved

Song Writer

A woman's worth is more cents than a dime
It shouldn't be taken for granted; only giving her small pieces of your time

A woman's worth is more cents than a nickel
Not to be played with by fickle people

A woman's worth is not for everyone to understand
But to be properly explained and presented through her man

A woman's worth cannot be felt in only one night
Even when she makes you feel like everything will turn out alright

A woman's worth is one of a kind
Not to be played with, not to toy with her mind

A woman's worth is patient and true
A woman's worth is made up of everything that surrounds you!

Daily Gratitude:

_____

_____

_____

_____

_____

_____.

Pleasure List For Today (Things to Do, Desires & Other Note(s)):

_____

_____

_____

_____

_____

_____.

Today's Affirmation:

_____

_____

_____

_____

_____

_____

_____.

Visualize Your Day:

_____

_____

_____

_____

_____

_____.

**Non-Pleasures of Today (Things to Do Tomorrow, Drama(s) of
The Day, Possible Failures & Do-Overs):**

_____

_____

_____

_____

_____

_____.

Reflections From Today:

_____

_____

_____

_____

_____

_____

_____.

Day 68

Affirmation: I Am Abundant

Love Letter To Myself

I love the way your voice sounds when you speak
As you remind me that I'm the only one you seek
You treat me like I'm the only one left on the peak
And you love me without showing that you're weak

I enjoy the way you make me feel complete
Makes me take a lighter step to the beat
Let me know you will never cheat
And this life hasn't turned out to be bittersweet

At first, I thought this was about you and me
Something to be televised but then I realized
I was in love with myself, completely in love…
….with my skin, my creativity,
My attractive body shape and my wealthy health

I love that way I love me…..
I love the taste of my sweet apologies
That I am now safe, loved, forgiven and complete
I love the way I turned out to be, the adult me

Daily Gratitude:

_____

_____

_____

_____

_____

_____.

Pleasure List For Today (Things to Do, Desires & Other Note(s)):

_____

_____

_____

_____

_____

_____.

Today's Affirmation:

_____

_____

_____

_____

_____

_____.

Visualize Your Day:

_____

_____

_____

_____

_____

_____.

Non-Pleasures of Today (Things to Do Tomorrow, Drama(s) of The Day, Possible Failures & Do-Overs):

_____

_____

_____

_____

_____

_____.

Reflections From Today:

_____

_____

_____

_____

_____

_____

_____.

Day 69
Affirmation:
I Am The Manager Of Me

Rapture # 37

A love so sweet that I have given it to myself
A love so unique, can't be filed away on a bookshelf
A love so sassy, it makes me want to approve of my own damn self
A love so pure, it brings out the best of one's mindset
A love so sensitive, it curls up to me like a bicep
A love so big,
It surpasses the amounts in my bank account and wealth status

A love so wide it must be multiplied…..
So, with this love that is the biggest of the biggest love
… and the deepest of the deepest of the deepest love
…and the purest of the purest of the purest of loves

I desire to take my journey
I desire to cross the multitudes of this love
And onto the multiple sides of loves
I desire to love as a guide
I desire to always have love by my side
I desire to love more
I desire to always adore….
ME

Rapture #37

Cont'd

I desire to break down this love and start with seven,
Multiple it by three,
Divide it by three
And bring back to seven

Hence, I deserve to represent my completeness, my holiness, my shine
At the perfect age of 37,
I am the perfection of both the physical and spiritual kind

I deserve to be flawless in my own nature
I deserve to have a love, a truth that it is able to seek and capture
I deserve to live as I am and as I explore
I deserve to erupt coming into my rapture evermore

Daily Gratitude:

_____

_____

_____

_____

_____

_____.

Pleasure List For Today (Things to Do, Desires & Other Note(s)):

_____

_____

_____

_____

_____

_____.

Today's Affirmation:

_____

_____

_____

_____

_____

_____

_____.

Visualize Your Day:

_____

_____

_____

_____

_____

_____.

Non-Pleasures of Today (Things to Do Tomorrow, Drama(s) of The Day, Possible Failures & Do-Overs):

_____

_____

_____

_____

_____

_____.

Reflections From Today:

_____

_____

_____

_____

_____

_____

_____.

Day 70
Affirmation: I Am Receptive
Teach Me How To Love You

I try to listen more but you're such a bore
And, when you speak, I get weak

In the worst possible way
It is so bad that I should not say

How your words don't affect me
And that my time spent with you
Doesn't allow me to be the best that I can be!

You say my words are too harsh
When I speak, you feel like you're sinking into a marsh

So I lighten my words, my actions and my thoughts
But instead of having make-up sex, we fought

We yelled and screamed and shouted at each other in disrespect
Then later, we're in deep thought and regret

Cause what we really wanted to do
Was teach each other how to love one another
But instead, we acted like we did not know each other

Teach Me How To Love You

Cont'd

In the streets, we didn't speak
In the sheet, I wasn't a freak
Over to your house, I hadn't been in the week
And my feelings were starting to feel bleak

I need to know where we went wrong
I want to know so we come out of this strong
I desire to feel love and to give it back in return
Teach me how to love you, I am willing to learn

Daily Gratitude:

_____

_____

_____

_____

_____

_____.

Pleasure List For Today (Things to Do, Desires & Other Note(s)):

_____

_____

_____

_____

_____

_____.

Today's Affirmation:

_____

_____

_____

_____

_____

_____

_____.

Visualize Your Day:

_____

_____

_____

_____

_____

_____.

Non-Pleasures of Today (Things to Do Tomorrow, Drama(s) of The Day, Possible Failures & Do-Overs):

_____

_____

_____

_____

_____

_____.

Reflections From Today:

_____

_____

_____

_____

_____

_____

_____.

Day 71
Affirmation: I Am Drama-Free

Life Is What You Make It

This rollercoaster ride has got me on a fantastic high.
I'm so high I can feel the hair move on my skin
From the pressure of the wind.
The wind is blowing fast against my face
As the rollercoaster begins to race
Down the hill and back up again.
Staying at a high steady pace…

This rollercoaster ride has got me on a fantastic high.
I'm so high I can smell the scent of hearts
Being broken when the news came to them fast,
Abruptly, like a rollercoaster crashing on its breaks.
And, the news read, hear ye… hear ye…. Read all about it…
We hear she's having another heartbreak
Cause she doesn't know when to say when….

This rollercoaster ride has got me on a fantastic high.
I'm so high I can hear the voices.
I can hear them loud and clear.
What I hear is the could-haves, would-haves and maybe I should have.
I cover my ears as the rollercoaster ride begins to go up the ladder.
The clicking sounds are causing me too much anxiety….

Life Is What You Make It

Cont'd

This rollercoaster ride has got me on a fantastic high....
Or does it?
Cause I'm so high I can hardly stand being on it anymore.
Just in time, I think of how my decision-making has been poor.
I look over my shoulder and I feel a pit in my stomach.
The rollercoaster has started to descend.
Got me thinking, is this the end?

This rollercoaster ride has got me on a messed-up kind of high.
As I descend from the sky, my eyes begin to cry.
I think of how my life could have been,
would have been and maybe should have been....
And at that moment, I jump off the rollercoaster ride

Because this rollercoaster ride ain't got me on no fantastic high.
Instead, I'm walking a pace and I have a stride.
Life is what I make it, not some uncontrollable rollercoaster ride.

And I'm loving me unconditionally!

Daily Gratitude:

_____
_____
_____
_____
_____
_____.

Pleasure List For Today (Things to Do, Desires & Other Note(s)):

_____
_____
_____
_____
_____.

Today's Affirmation:

_____
_____
_____
_____
_____
_____.

Visualize Your Day:

_____

_____

_____

_____

_____

_____.

Non-Pleasures of Today (Things to Do Tomorrow, Drama(s) of The Day, Possible Failures & Do-Overs):

_____

_____

_____

_____

_____

_____.

Reflections From Today:

_____

_____

_____

_____

_____

_____.

Day 72
Affirmation: I Am Drug-Free

Don't Look

Don't look too hard at my face
Remembering what you said about us moving at a slower pace

You had it but you didn't know what to do
So now I'm singing that old love song right back to you

Don't look too hard at my sexy waist
Looking further down and remembering how it taste

No more hugs and kisses goodbye
No more helping you, no more wondering why?

Don't look so closely at the new ring on my finger
You had your chance and you chose neither

Don't look too hard at the dip in my lower back
Just make sure that all of your bags are packed

Don't look too hard at my door keys, new car or huge bank account
No more wondering what we were all about

So don't look too hard at the past and our love
Because it has been taken away by a black dove

Daily Gratitude:

_____

_____

_____

_____

_____

_____.

Pleasure List For Today (Things to Do, Desires & Other Note(s)):

_____

_____

_____

_____

_____

_____.

Today's Affirmation:

_____

_____

_____

_____

_____

_____

_____.

Visualize Your Day:

_____
_____
_____
_____
_____
_____.

Non-Pleasures of Today (Things to Do Tomorrow, Drama(s) of The Day, Possible Failures & Do-Overs):

_____
_____
_____
_____
_____
_____.

Reflections From Today:

_____
_____
_____
_____
_____
_____.

Day 73
Affirmation: I Am Alcohol-Free

Did I Get In My Own Way?

I had something special and now it's gone
I had something sweet and then it got weak
I had the truth but it soon became a lie
And now there's no more condensation coming from the sky
This level of loss could lead to hills of frustration
However, this level of change has sparked my elevation
This level of change will lead to my graduation
This level of evolution is my revelation

Daily Gratitude:

_____
_____
_____
_____
_____
_____.

Pleasure List For Today (Things to Do, Desires & Other Note(s)):

_____
_____
_____
_____
_____
_____.

Today's Affirmation:

_____
_____
_____
_____
_____
_____
_____.

Visualize Your Day:

_____

_____

_____

_____

_____

_____.

Non-Pleasures of Today (Things to Do Tomorrow, Drama(s) of The Day, Possible Failures & Do-Overs):

_____

_____

_____

_____

_____

_____.

Reflections From Today:

_____

_____

_____

_____

_____

_____

_____.

Day 74
Affirmation: I Am Toxic-Free

One More

So that I could say all that I needed to say

All I needed was one more hour
To show you that I was the one with all the power

All I needed was one more second
To know that I shouldn't been at your every call or beckon

All I needed was one more minute
To let you know that you will never understand it

Now all that I need is one more line
To realize that you were never really mine

Daily Gratitude:

_____

_____

_____

_____

_____

_____.

Pleasure List For Today (Things to Do, Desires & Other Note(s)):

_____

_____

_____

_____

_____

_____.

Today's Affirmation:

_____

_____

_____

_____

_____

_____

_____.

Visualize Your Day:

_____

_____

_____

_____

_____

_____.

Non-Pleasures of Today (Things to Do Tomorrow, Drama(s) of The Day, Possible Failures & Do-Overs):

_____

_____

_____

_____

_____

_____.

Reflections From Today:

_____

_____

_____

_____

_____

_____.

Day 75
Affirmation: I Am Capable

Not Again

How could I let this happen again
Me thinking of him with my fingers rapidly tapping

As I tap, I blink one eye
Reminding myself that I wasn't supposed to cry

I thought he was different
Someone to make me happy

I thought he was the one
Someone my children could call Pappy

What happened to our late-night phone calls?
What happened to us holding hands while walking through the mall?

I just can't understand how this is happening again….
And, whenever I see you, you always have a grin
On your face!

Maybe that was a sign
When you held me and said that I was on your mind
Not again...

I just can't take it anymore
I just can't stand to be another's man play toy
Not again

Daily Gratitude:

_____
_____
_____
_____
_____
_____.

Pleasure List For Today (Things to Do, Desires & Other Note(s)):

_____
_____
_____
_____
_____
_____.

Today's Affirmation:

_____
_____
_____
_____
_____
_____.

Visualize Your Day:

_____

_____

_____

_____

_____

_____.

Non-Pleasures of Today (Things to Do Tomorrow, Drama(s) of The Day, Possible Failures & Do-Overs):

_____

_____

_____

_____

_____

_____.

Reflections From Today:

_____

_____

_____

_____

_____

_____

_____.

Day 76
Affirmation: I Am Hopeful

Why Do Bad Boys
Want Good Girls

I guess it really does mean something
When your mother says stay away from that boy
Because what he is about is up to no good
I had a male friend
The type you could not bring home to your mother
The type that would influence you to be his girl
The type that said that I was not like any other

The type that says he'll take care of you
The type that calls you late at night
The type that always calls you his boo
The type that tries to do everything that's right
But it seems as though things never work out that way
He turns in the wrong direction
And ends up in jail or somewhere else leading him astray

It happened all in one summer.
The year that was made for just us two
We exchanged kisses and hugs
I played in his hair as he told me his secrets
Secrets that only I knew, just between him and me
He trusted me with all his heart
That I would not be the one to play him like a fool again
It's a wonder…

Why Do Bad Boy
Want Good Girls

Cont'd

How much faith, love and guidance you can give to a person
He looked to me as a friend, as a counselor
That I would be there until the end
He eventually made it to jail that same summer
And that's where he stayed
Which was a huge bummer

As the days went pass, I remembered the times we spent together
Lying in his bed, side by side,
Watching a movie or just listening to the radio
Something that I will always remember…..

He always reminded me that I was the only one for him
How he could never say, "I love you' to someone else
Who was never there for him
I now sit back and wonder
If I would have said, "Yes" to him that day
To be his girl and only one, I could be with him this day
Six feet underground
Letting my soul wander without a body
Thinking about how I could not say goodbye
How he left so suddenly without a tear to cry and a word to say

As I grieved...
I knew that was not the end of a friendship that I held near
Close to my heart and in my book
Where I wrote this art piece
And holding back my one last tear.

Daily Gratitude:

_____

_____

_____

_____

_____

_____ .

Pleasure List For Today (Things to Do, Desires & Other Note(s)):

_____

_____

_____

_____

_____

_____ .

Today's Affirmation:

_____

_____

_____

_____

_____

_____

_____ .

Visualize Your Day:

_____

_____

_____

_____

_____

_____.

Non-Pleasures of Today (Things to Do Tomorrow, Drama(s) of The Day, Possible Failures & Do-Overs):

_____

_____

_____

_____

_____

_____.

Reflections From Today:

_____

_____

_____

_____

_____

_____

_____.

Day 77
Affirmation: I Attract Wealth

Emotions

Controlling my emotions is all up to me
Controlling my emotions is a representation of who I want to be

It's not the responsibility of no one else in the world
If I choose to let my feelings roll around and twirl

Out of control like I no longer want to live
Cause that would only leave me deprived and unable to forgive

What I need most, is my sanity and will to live
To thrive, not only survive and to feel 100% alive

Daily Gratitude:

_____
_____
_____
_____
_____
_____.

Pleasure List For Today (Things to Do, Desires & Other Note(s)):

_____
_____
_____
_____
_____
_____.

Today's Affirmation:

_____
_____
_____
_____
_____
_____
_____.

Visualize Your Day:

_____

_____

_____

_____

_____

_____.

Non-Pleasures of Today (Things to Do Tomorrow, Drama(s) of The Day, Possible Failures & Do-Overs):

_____

_____

_____

_____

_____

_____.

Reflections From Today:

_____

_____

_____

_____

_____

_____

_____.

Day 78
Affirmation: I Am Confident

My Little Garden

I worked in my garden on today
And my my my…what a special place that I have manifested my way

My fruits and veggies are growing nice and strong
All growing in my little garden, protected and loved,
Nothing can go wrong

The bees buzz around them, pollinating them, as they should
The deer looking over my fence, thinking about coming in,
And I wish they would

But I know they won't cause my little garden is not for them
As my little garden will never be condemned

How grateful I am for this newly found joy
A place to play in the dirt, like a kid with a new toy

My little garden not only gives life
But also a sanctuary for my sanity and peace
My little garden, with so much life and wealth,
Growing without any reason to cease

As the sky waters them, they grow
As I tend to them, my health and wealth continue to flow

I worked in my little garden on today
And all I can say is I'm blessed for each renewing day

Daily Gratitude:

_____
_____
_____
_____
_____
_____.

Pleasure List For Today (Things to Do, Desires & Other Note(s)):

_____
_____
_____
_____
_____
_____.

Today's Affirmation:

_____
_____
_____
_____
_____
_____
_____.

Visualize Your Day:

_____

_____

_____

_____

_____

_____.

Non-Pleasures of Today (Things to Do Tomorrow, Drama(s) of The Day, Possible Failures & Do-Overs):

_____

_____

_____

_____

_____

_____.

Reflections From Today:

_____

_____

_____

_____

_____

_____

_____.

Day 79
Affirmation:
I Am An Entrepreneur

Fun & Pleasure

I write these words with desire to change the world
I have the title of bestselling author
And when I walk through the room, heads swirl
My life's experiences, all coming together, beautifully unfurled
And I desire to take on this world, just watch me uncurl

I write these words with desire to sell out
My artwork within the first week
Nothing to be negative about or make things seem bleak
My world travels may make me feel tired and weak
Yet I know people are waiting to hear me speak

I desire to travel the world speaking about my books
Wear fancy clothes, eat healthy tasty foods
And have enough money to hire a private cook
To see amazing sights under the moonlight;
Have irreplaceable life experiences, oh my…what a look
I am a wealthy woman, who knew?
I am a healer, unshaken by my schedule that's fully booked

I am a self-made millionaire, an entrepreneur, a sista and a mother
I am a goddess, a Queen and an amazing lover
I am blessed, I am grateful and no need to be anything other

Daily Gratitude:

_____

_____

_____

_____

_____

_____.

Pleasure List For Today (Things to Do, Desires & Other Note(s)):

_____

_____

_____

_____

_____

_____.

Today's Affirmation:

_____

_____

_____

_____

_____

_____

_____.

Visualize Your Day:

_____

_____

_____

_____

_____

_____.

Non-Pleasures of Today (Things to Do Tomorrow, Drama(s) of The Day, Possible Failures & Do-Overs):

_____

_____

_____

_____

_____

_____.

Reflections From Today:

_____

_____

_____

_____

_____

_____

_____.

Day 80
Affirmation: I Have Discernment

Proudness

I am so proud of me
As I am turning out exactly how I thought I would be
I gave myself the gift of loving me
And in return, I have a brand new level of self-expectancy

I accepted myself just as I was
Not doing things just because
I am finally saying YES to me
I upgraded myself and found contentment in just being me

I wear happiness and serenity as my crown
Now every time I wear it, it makes me proud
Of my growth, my ability to shine and my skin so brown
My ability to stand out in the middle of a crowd

I am love, I am peace, I am serenity and I am joy
I am timeless, I am ageless, I am someone I enjoy

Daily Gratitude:

_____
_____
_____
_____
_____
_____.

Pleasure List For Today (Things to Do, Desires & Other Note(s)):

_____
_____
_____
_____
_____
_____.

Today's Affirmation:

_____
_____
_____
_____
_____
_____
_____.

Visualize Your Day:

_____

_____

_____

_____

_____

_____.

Non-Pleasures of Today (Things to Do Tomorrow, Drama(s) of The Day, Possible Failures & Do-Overs):

_____

_____

_____

_____

_____

_____.

Reflections From Today:

_____

_____

_____

_____

_____

_____

_____.

Day 81
Affirmation: I Am A Healer
A Vow To Myself

I vow to be a goddess first
I vow to love myself the most,
To be nice to myself not to think of the worst
I vow to forgive myself no matter how big or small the mistake is
I vow to remember I know best, I am a wiz
I vow to live in my faith
As my life unfolds in mysterious divine perfection
I vow to honor my spiritual path
And create an amazing life utilizing self-protection
I vow to live a life that is true to my arts, talent, creativity and skills
I vow to enjoy my endless wisdom
And excellent memory that comes with all of life's frills

Daily Gratitude:

_____

_____

_____

_____

_____

_____.

Pleasure List For Today (Things to Do, Desires & Other Note(s)):

_____

_____

_____

_____

_____

_____.

Today's Affirmation:

_____

_____

_____

_____

_____

_____

_____.

Visualize Your Day:

_____

_____

_____

_____

_____

_____.

Non-Pleasures of Today (Things to Do Tomorrow, Drama(s) of The Day, Possible Failures & Do-Overs):

_____

_____

_____

_____

_____

_____.

Reflections From Today:

_____

_____

_____

_____

_____

_____

_____.

Day 82
Affirmation: I Am Loyal

Burdened No More

I was burdened with my mother's, my grandmother's
And her mother's dream
I had lost the taste for eating ice cream
When the pressure was applied on how life should be lived as an adult
Anything that went wrong felt like it was all my fault

Thinking of everything they were not
One of their dreams was to complete college, not sit around and rot
So I did, I went to college and made others happy and smile
I finished it fast and tired yet accomplished
Feeling like I ran three thousand miles

I received my master's degree, became highly educated and married
But for that last part, I needed a magical fairy
I didn't know what to do with my very own man
I did not know it would feel so awkward just to hold his hand

I wasn't use to public displays of affection
Now that I'm older, I can understand that type of connection
Unfortunately, the lesson was learned a little too late
But no worries, it's not so bad going on a blind date

For I am burdened no more with the dream of my ancestors of my past
For my future is looking brighter
And there's no rain in my future's forecast

Daily Gratitude:

_____

_____

_____

_____

_____

_____.

Pleasure List For Today (Things to Do, Desires & Other Note(s)):

_____

_____

_____

_____

_____

_____.

Today's Affirmation:

_____

_____

_____

_____

_____

_____

_____.

Visualize Your Day:

_____

_____

_____

_____

_____

_____.

Non-Pleasures of Today (Things to Do Tomorrow, Drama(s) of The Day, Possible Failures & Do-Overs):

_____

_____

_____

_____

_____

_____.

Reflections From Today:

_____

_____

_____

_____

_____

_____

_____.

Day 83
Affirmation: I Am Positivity

Break-A-way

When I decided to break-a-way
From their ideas of what life should be
I decided to go and follow my own soul's adventure for me

They felt I was the betrayer, a lost soul I would be
Funny shit, I felt I was betrayed, for it was them, not me

I didn't quite know where my soul's adventure would lead me
So I said a prayer, removed my resistance and just let it be

They said I had become self-absorbed meaning
I was only thinking of me
That was just the opposite…
I just wasn't sure of who I wanted to be

Maybe there was some unrealistic meaning of my life's goals
And who I really wanted to be
Maybe what I wanted was unattainable
But it wasn't their choice and they should have just let me be me

Instead of being mislabeled…
Or told that I was acting self-absorbed,
Not like the old version of me
I should have been viewed as awakened
Because that is all I wanted to be

So, when I finally did get to break away
From their ideas of what life should be
I was happy that I did not completely lose myself
I was finally being the original version of me

Daily Gratitude:

_____
_____
_____
_____
_____
_____.

Pleasure List For Today (Things to Do, Desires & Other Note(s)):

_____
_____
_____
_____
_____
_____.

Today's Affirmation:

_____
_____
_____
_____
_____
_____
_____.

Visualize Your Day:

_____

_____

_____

_____

_____

_____.

Non-Pleasures of Today (Things to Do Tomorrow, Drama(s) of The Day, Possible Failures & Do-Overs):

_____

_____

_____

_____

_____

_____.

Reflections From Today:

_____

_____

_____

_____

_____

_____.

Day 84
Affirmation: I Am Accepted

Awakening

In my awakening, I knew the world had two entrances
One entrance led to my happiness
And the other leads to pleasing others

I was seeking to find my happiness in theirs
And pleasing others made my soul cry
It was daunting to follow others' dreams
And trying to do so sucked me dry

I knew following others would only make me feel sick
I didn't like, not one bit
I became a bigger and bolder rebel
Because I had no desire to follow others
Following others would make me feel caged and smothered

Consequently, I was led into a dreadful burnout
A very dark place where the lights are always out

I hated that experience of a burnout,
I was constantly crying and wanting to shout

I prayed for my awakening, a horizon of some sort
And in my awakening,
I became a leader and builder of a peaceful fort

And as a leader,
I arose phoenix style, unleashed and untamed
Promising myself to never again become that drained

Daily Gratitude:

_____

_____

_____

_____

_____

_____.

Pleasure List For Today (Things to Do, Desires & Other Note(s)):

_____

_____

_____

_____

_____

_____.

Today's Affirmation:

_____

_____

_____

_____

_____

_____

_____.

Visualize Your Day:

_____

_____

_____

_____

_____

_____.

Non-Pleasures of Today (Things to Do Tomorrow, Drama(s) of The Day, Possible Failures & Do-Overs):

_____

_____

_____

_____

_____

_____.

Reflections From Today:

_____

_____

_____

_____

_____

_____.

Day 85
Affirmation: I Am Awesomeness

Beautiful Mess

Life can be a beautiful mess
Life can feel unwanted if you focus on less
For me, life has been a beautiful sight
And life has allowed me to see the light

I've remained in my know
Knowing how to speak and how to move
Yet others tried to sway me left and right
I have managed to remain leveled-headed and tight

Tight and true to myself
And all of the desires of my heart
I have desired to learn from all of my experiences
And from that, I have made my life a piece of art

Daily Gratitude:

_____

_____

_____

_____

_____

_____

Pleasure List For Today (Things to Do, Desires & Other Note(s)):

_____

_____

_____

_____

_____

_____

Today's Affirmation:

_____

_____

_____

_____

_____

_____

_____

Visualize Your Day:

_____

_____

_____

_____

_____

_____.

Non-Pleasures of Today (Things to Do Tomorrow, Drama(s) of The Day, Possible Failures & Do-Overs):

_____

_____

_____

_____

_____

_____.

Reflections From Today:

_____

_____

_____

_____

_____

_____

_____

_____.

Day 86
Affirmation: I Am Conscience

Back & Better

I am stronger and I am wiser
I am healthier than before
I am a goddess, I am a Queen
People look and all adore

I am sensual, I am more
Than anything you could think of
I am renewed, I am abundance
People try but can't ignore

I am strong, I love to explore
I am well diverse and have a sense of self
I am an overcomer, I am a lover
I am entertaining, never a bore

I am desired, I am beautiful
People stare when I walk through the door
I am her, I am royalty
Overflowing with grace, leaving my people wanting more

Daily Gratitude:

_____

_____

_____

_____

_____

_____.

Pleasure List For Today (Things to Do, Desires & Other Note(s)):

_____

_____

_____

_____

_____

_____.

Today's Affirmation:

_____

_____

_____

_____

_____

_____.

Visualize Your Day:

_____

_____

_____

_____

_____

_____.

Non-Pleasures of Today (Things to Do Tomorrow, Drama(s) of The Day, Possible Failures & Do-Overs):

_____

_____

_____

_____

_____

_____.

Reflections From Today:

_____

_____

_____

_____

_____

_____

_____.

Day 87
Affirmation: I Am Radiant

Lioness

I became the lioness of this jungle called life
I put on my armor to deal with life's strife

I looked at everything as if it was my lunch
I paddle my heart when encountering someone's sucker punch

And soon I arrived at my seat at a table fit for a goddess
It was there that I took my rightful place with grace and modest

My thoughts filled my plate as I ate with exclusivity
I consumed joy, peace, creativity

It was a renewal of my mind, spirit and soul
There was also abundance, wealth, and health that filled my bowl

I increased my financial stability,
Positive belief system and optimistic attitude
I spoke quietly while I expanded my support system,
Self-discipline and self-love with no need to allude

For I had embraced my lioness role in this jungle called life
With my intelligence, positive self-expression of me
And so much more to look forward to in my afterlife

Daily Gratitude:

_____

_____

_____

_____

_____

_____.

Pleasure List For Today (Things to Do, Desires & Other Note(s)):

_____

_____

_____

_____

_____

_____.

Today's Affirmation:

_____

_____

_____

_____

_____

_____.

Visualize Your Day:

_____

_____

_____

_____

_____

_____

Non-Pleasures of Today (Things to Do Tomorrow, Drama(s) of The Day, Possible Failures & Do-Overs):

_____

_____

_____

_____

_____

_____

Reflections From Today:

_____

_____

_____

_____

_____

_____

_____

Day 88
Affirmation: I Believe In Me

I Am Me

What an amazing place to be
To rediscover the goddess in me

To have my own space with security
Knowing everything I have gained is blessed with purity

What an amazing person I have grown to be
To rediscover the goddess in me

To own my own peace
To provide for myself without major decrease

What an amazing future is coming to me
To rediscover the goddess in me

To master myself, to fight for me
Losing my goddess again, never will come to be

Daily Gratitude:

_____

_____

_____

_____

_____

_____.

Pleasure List For Today (Things to Do, Desires & Other Note(s)):

_____

_____

_____

_____

_____

_____.

Today's Affirmation:

_____

_____

_____

_____

_____

_____

_____.

Visualize Your Day:

_____

_____

_____

_____

_____

_____.

Non-Pleasures of Today (Things to Do Tomorrow, Drama(s) of The Day, Possible Failures & Do-Overs):

_____

_____

_____

_____

_____

_____.

Reflections From Today:

_____

_____

_____

_____

_____

_____

_____.

At the end of my eighty-eight days, my routine was booming with high vibrations and positive vibes. There was consistency and productivity within me. I was grateful and looking forward to the next time to relax, as well as, refocus and rejuvenate myself. How do you feel?

_____

_____

_____

_____

_____

_____ .

_____

_____

_____

_____

_____

_____

_____ .

It is my desire that you find this practice beneficial just as I have. After my eighty-eight days of journaling, I was walking, surviving, thriving and peaceful. I was managing stress and anxiety well, in my opinion, and when small barriers arose, I tackled them without any major disruptions to my life. I was proud of myself with a greater sense of self-appreciation and self-awareness. Most of all, I am proud of you for taking this journey. Don't forget, we can always rediscover the goddess through our own journaling journey.

Sending peace, renewed strength and love your way!

About the Author

In high school, I chose I Know Why The Caged Bird Sings by Maya Angelou, for a book report. This book is an unforgettable autobiography detailing the strength, courage, and wisdom of an amazing black woman. I researched why a caged bird may sing:

1. Struggle
2. Unfair treatment
3. Unrest in the soul

For me, I experienced all three - an internal struggle of wanting to be it all: a mother, wife, entrepreneur, daughter, sister, best friend, employee, world traveler, and explorer all while being untamed. There was a sense of unfair treatment within the patriarchal world that demonstrated an imbalance among gender roles inside and outside of the home. In addition to the unrest in my soul breeding resentment that rose from me having more workloads and fewer playdates in my life, year after year. With so many responsibilities, I felt like I was losing my sense of self. So what did I do, I rediscovered my goddess.

And now, I ask myself, what can't this goddess do? How does this goddess learn how to start self-loving herself again? Simple, she reunites with herself. She carefully and strategically navigates from relationships with others into a relationship with herself. In doing so, she believes she can, so she does it! She trusts everything will work in her favor, and it does!

Rediscovering the goddess in me demonstrates the recreation of goddess-like habits and routines to restore and rejuvenate one's self through journaling. Within these pages, I provide you, the reader, a space to create your personal daily practices as you acknowledge, accept, discover, and rediscover the goddess in you.

In understanding how to love, unlove and love again, this book provides the reader with the space to capture the journey from rupture to rapture.